Key Concepts in Measurement

POCKET GUIDES TO
SOCIAL WORK RESEARCH METHODS

Series Editor
Tony Tripodi, DSW
Professor Emeritus, Ohio State University

BRIAN E. PERRON
DAVID F. GILLESPIE

Key Concepts in Measurement

OXFORD
UNIVERSITY PRESS

OXFORD
UNIVERSITY PRESS

Oxford University Press is a department of the University of
Oxford. It furthers the University's objective of excellence in research,
scholarship, and education by publishing worldwide.

Oxford   New York
Auckland   Cape Town   Dar es Salaam   Hong Kong   Karachi
Kuala Lumpur   Madrid   Melbourne   Mexico City   Nairobi
New Delhi   Shanghai   Taipei   Toronto

With offices in
Argentina   Austria   Brazil   Chile   Czech Republic   France   Greece
Guatemala   Hungary   Italy   Japan   Poland   Portugal   Singapore
South Korea   Switzerland   Thailand   Turkey   Ukraine   Vietnam

Oxford is a registered trademark of Oxford University Press
in the UK and certain other countries.

Published in the United States of America by
Oxford University Press
198 Madison Avenue, New York, NY 10016

Library of Congress Cataloging-in-Publication Data
Gillespie, David F.
Key Concepts in Measurement / David F. Gillespie and Brian E. Perron.
pages cm. — (Pocket guides to social work research methods)
Includes bibliographical references and index.
ISBN 978-0-19-985548-3 (alk. paper)
1. Social service—Research—Methodology.   I. Perron, Brian E.   II. Title.
HV11.G48 2015
361.0072—dc23
2014031216

1 3 5 7 9 8 6 4 2
Printed in the United States of America
on acid-free paper

Contents

Key Concepts in Measurement

1

Introduction

Accurate and minute measurement seems to the non-scientific imagination, a less lofty and dignified work than looking for something new. But nearly all the grandest discoveries of science have been but the rewards of accurate measurement and patient long-continued labour in the minute sifting of numerical results.

—Baron William Thomson Kelvin (1871)

One of the great mistakes is to judge policies and programs by their intentions rather than their results.

—Milton Friedman (1975)

In general, measurement refers to the process of assigning a numeric value to, or ordering characteristics or traits of, entities under study, so ideally the labels represent accurately the characteristic measured. Measurement is necessary for building and testing theory, specifying problems, and defining goals (Corcoran & Fischer, 2000). It is arguably one of the most important and difficult tasks in social work research.

In the classic text *Basic Dilemmas in the Social Sciences*, Blalock (1984) argues:

> [M]easurement problems in the social sciences are formidable.... A very complex auxiliary measurement theory is often needed in the social sciences to understand this linkage problem. Our present knowledge as to how to construct and analyze data with such measurement models is developing, but it is not yet sufficient to provide really definitive guidelines for measurement. In effect, measurement problems produce a host of unknowns that must be added to those involved in one's substantive theory. (p. 18)

Although this argument was made more than 35 years ago, the relevance and importance of measurement in social work remains. For example, Feldman and Siskind (1997) state that the current attacks on human service organizations are not based on empirical data, but rather the absence of reliable data. Ultimately, effective measurement is essential to overcoming this problem. Recent research has shown existing problems involved in the development and validation of social work measures (Guo, Perron, & Gillespie, 2008), in addition to other broad criticisms of social work journal quality (Sellers, Mathesien, Perry, & Smith, 2004; Society for Social Work and Research, 2005). Social work researchers who are not expert in developing, selecting, and using measures will not be able to contribute maximally to the social work knowledge base. Such knowledge and skills related to measurement ultimately determine the extent to which social work research can inform social policy and social work interventions effectively. This book serves as a guide for developing, selecting, and using measures in social work research.

DOES MEASUREMENT MATTER?

Measurement is an integral part of modern living. We depend on measurement to a considerable extent. Measuring devices are so commonplace and pervasive that it is surprising we forget how much of our day relies on or is affected by measurements. We hang clocks on the wall and wear a watch on our wrist to keep track of time. We keep a scale in the bathroom to check our weight. Thermometers are mounted both indoors and outside to give us temperature readings. Items we purchase often include the weight of the contents. Various gauges and meters are installed in our cars to help monitor speed, the amount of gas in the tank, oil pressure, engine temperature, miles driven, and so on. The number of measuring devices used today is immense and increasing. These and many more measuring instruments are providing continuous information that we use to make decisions. Without such information, our ability to do things would be greatly hampered.

A byproduct of this pervasive use of measuring devices is our presumed confidence in their accuracy. To a large extent, this confidence is justified—especially when applied to pressure gauges, clocks, thermometers, and other physical measuring instruments. These instruments facilitate safety, efficiency, and comfort. Extensive checks are made by the federal government and other organizations to maintain accurate measuring instruments. The U.S. Bureau of Standards, among its other activities, maintains the standards against which instruments for measuring distance and weight can be checked. Other governmental officials conduct regular checks of commonly used measuring devices such as the scales used in grocery stores and meters used in gasoline stations. Similarly, researchers are constantly recalibrating the thermometers, burettes (graduated glass tubes with a valve at the bottom used for measuring a liquid or gas), and weights used in the physical sciences and engineering to be certain that accuracy is maintained.

Measurement in the social sciences in general—and social work specifically—has not yet achieved the degree of standardization characteristic of the physical sciences. In the field of physical science, many of the factors that affect measurement readings have already been identified and can be eliminated or minimized through adjustments, at least enough so that a measurement reading by one scientist can be verified independently by others. In social research, many of the variables that affect measurement have not been identified and, of those that have, we find they often resist control or elimination. The checkmark on a census taker's protocol, for example, is in part a function of the specific question asked—income, marital status, number of children—and in part a function of social circumstances, such as the interviewer's appearance, the respondent's relations to the law, neighbors, bill collectors, and so forth. Responses to questions about job satisfaction are, no doubt, a function of satisfaction to a certain degree, but they are also a function of the respondent's language comprehension, relations with the employing organization and supervisor, ethnic or cultural differences in the use of positive and negative adjectives, and many other possibilities. Despite the differences in standardization, there is increasing use of educational, psychological, and social measurement to help us make decisions. Aptitude and achievement tests, and various psychological inventories are now in widespread use at all levels of education. Skill tests and attitude scales are used frequently for employment screening. Various screening devices can help identify persons who have a mental disorder. The use of honesty tests is expanding in banking, retailing, and other industries in which opportunities for deceit and fraud are inherent in the work. Tenure and promotion decisions of social work researchers are often based on impact, which requires clarity on the definition and the measurement of this important concept. The research on risk and protective factors has helped us understand who is likely to drop out of school, allowing social workers to target scarce resources more effectively—an area of study that requires sound measurement.

As we stop to think about these measurements, it is clear they, too, have become woven into the fabric of modern living. Although the measurement of psychological, educational, and social phenomena is less firm than the measurement of physical phenomena, the presumed confidence in measurement is carried over by many people, including researchers and professionals, and applied in good faith to measures of mental abilities, self-esteem, honesty, marital satisfaction, and other concepts studied by social scientists. Sometimes this confidence is justified; other times it is not.

An understanding of how measures in social research are developed and constructed is essential to evaluating the worth of any social research. If a study bases its conclusions either all or in part on measures that are inappropriate, out of date, or of dubious validity, the research—even if executed adequately—will present conclusions that are suspect. Being able to recognize good measurement and make use of it is important in modern society, both in our personal and professional lives.

THE PURPOSE OF THIS BOOK

The purpose of this book is twofold. First, we take the opportunity to review key concepts in social work measurement. The area of social measurement is vast, so it is impossible to provide a comprehensive review of all the concepts. In fact, because measurement is intertwined so deeply with both theory and statistics, it would be impossible to cover every topic in a single volume, particularly a handbook. The key concepts we choose to review are those that seem to give rise to a number of problems we have observed in social work research literature. For example, although Cronbach's alpha is one of the most commonly used statistics for assessing reliability in general—and internal consistency, in particular—its interpretation is widely misunderstood as a property of the measure itself. Similarly, factor analytic studies abound in the social work literature. Although software innovations have made such studies easy to conduct, churning out a range of statistics for model assessment, it is often the case that very little attention is paid to the conceptual and theoretical aspects of the measure—and the conceptual and theoretical aspects ultimately determine the measure's worth. For example, many of the factor analytic studies published in social work journals lack clear definitional boundaries around the concepts that articulate the domain from which the items were derived. Thus, a number of the concepts we review provide a backdrop for helping one understand many of the problems that are barriers to the advancement of social work measurement.

The second purpose of this book is to help update social work's knowledge base with respect to recent and important developments in measurement. This approach may seem a bit peculiar, particularly because numerous texts already cover topics such as validity, reliability, latent variables, and other important issues. The issue of whether enough new knowledge exists to warrant an update on various measurement topics is legitimate. We certainly think there is. For example, the most important topic area we seek to update is the theoretical understanding of validity. Currently, the field of social work labors under an outdated view by defining validity based on the question: Does the instrument measure what it is intended to measure? From the standpoint of contemporary validity theory, this is not the question that we should be asking. More specifically, one of the most important contemporary definitions of validity is provided by Messick (1989): "Validity is an integrated evaluative judgment of the degree to which empirical evidence and theoretical rationales support the *adequacy* and *appropriateness* of *inferences* and *actions* based on test scores or other modes of assessment" (italics in original; p. 13). This definition is far more than a simple change of wording. This new definition gives rise to differences in the ways we should think about, collect, and interpret validity evidence. Our chapter on validity theory (Chapter 3) provides a more detailed discussion of contemporary validity theory.

The measurement literature is extremely large, which makes the selection of topics to be included a challenge. We faced significant opportunity costs in each section of this handbook. That is, by devoting attention to one topic necessarily requires the exclusion of something else. Our general approach to the selection of topics was to reflect some of the most commonly encountered and most problematic measurement issues found in social work research. For example, we purposefully devote attention to issues of measuring latent variables because of their ubiquity in social work research. Latent variables are variables that are hidden from direct observation or they are hypothetical constructs hypothesized to facilitate scientific explanation. Within this area, we gave more attention to factor analysis compared with other modeling approaches (e.g., latent-class analysis, mixture models, item response theory [IRT], and generalizability theory [or G-theory]), given that factor analysis is the dominant approach to latent-variable analysis in social work research. Our selection of topics should not be interpreted as how the research enterprise ought to be. Instead, the selection of issues is to help sort out many of the problems commonly encountered in the research we do.

FOR WHOM THIS BOOK IS INTENDED

Measurement is the foundation of all empirical research. The advancement of any topic in social work research necessarily requires sound measurement practices. Some prior exposure to research methods and multivariate statistics is necessary to understand and appreciate more fully the advanced topics covered, such as contemporary validity theory, reliability, and latent-variable modeling. Thus, for doctoral students, this book should be a supplement to a research methods course or, ideally, part of an entire course devoted specifically to measurement. As mentioned, one of the objectives of this book is to provide an update to our social work research knowledge base, making it broadly relevant to social work researchers.

ORGANIZATION AND USE OF THIS HANDBOOK

To use this book effectively, we recommend you do a quick scan of it to get a sense of its general organization. This overview will help you identify the issues or points that have immediate relevance. We worked to present sufficient detail to guide you; however, the amount of detail presented may represent only a small portion of the literature to explicate the points fully. Providing all the necessary detail is not possible, particularly because entire books, special issues of journals, and papers have been devoted to the theoretical, technical, and practical aspects of measurement. Thus, we encourage you to review the readings that conclude each chapter. We refer to them as *suggested* and *classic readings*. They are suggested readings because they provide additional elaboration of the topics covered in each chapter. We also include a number of classic readings. Although some of these readings may not represent the contemporary views of the various topics, they reveal important developments at the time, thereby providing you with important historical information to understand more fully how the various topics have evolved over time. We are confident that such a historical understanding will help enrich your understanding of contemporary views.

This first chapter (Chapter 1) serves as a launch pad for the handbook. Although it does not address any special measurement topics specifically, it contains a number of important generalities for understanding our strategy in the selection and presentation of the various topics that follow. Chapter 2 is a refresher of both measurement concepts and theory, and is necessary for understanding many of the measurement complexities presented in later chapters.

We consider Chapter 3 to be the most important part of the book, for two reasons. First, it covers the topic of validity, which is the most critical of every conceivable measurement issue. Second, it provides an important update to the field's understanding of what validity is and is not. The ultimate goal of Chapter 3 is to convince social work researchers to adopt a contemporary understanding of validity. This contemporary understanding of validity has become common knowledge in other fields, particularly psychology and education, but has yet to penetrate the field of social work. Chapter 4 updates our understanding of reliability and addresses specific issues and problems related to reliability that are common to many different research efforts in social work.

In Chapter 5 we give focused attention to latent variables. This particular topic was selected because many, if not most, of the variables studied in social work can (or should) be regarded as latent variables. Numerous books and articles can be found on the empirical aspects of latent-variable modeling, covering topics such as selection and interpretation of fit indices, methods of estimation, and model selection. Our approach to latent-variable modeling is different; we focus attention on conceptual and theoretical issues of latent variables, which tend to receive far less attention in the social work literature, although the conceptual and theoretical issues are, primarily and demonstrably, more important than the empirical ones.

Chapter 6 examines issues related to publishing. Thus, it provides practical guidance on improving our writing on topics of measurement, and promotes more rigorous reviews. Chapter 6 is followed by a glossary of key concepts that appear throughout the book. A strong understanding of these concepts is essential to conducting theoretically informed empirical social work research. We encourage doctoral students to review these concepts carefully to build their overall fund of measurement knowledge.

COMMENTS ON CRITERIA, GUIDELINES, AND THRESHOLDS

Many aspects of measurement lend themselves to criteria, guidelines, or thresholds for determining the acceptability, or goodness, of a measure. Numerous publications that provide criteria and guidelines are cited for many of the topics discussed in this handbook. This is especially true for interpretations of validity and reliability coefficients, item and model selection in factor analysis, and sample size requirements for various procedures. Unfortunately, published criteria and guidelines can be ambiguous and sometimes contradictory, which gives researchers considerable freedom to justify a wide range of measurement decisions, some of which may appear opportunistic.

In the spirit of writing a *handbook*, we offer what is better regarded as principles and strategies, as opposed to a "cookbook" or a set of rules. These principles and strategies are intended to be a starting point for helping you sort through important measurement decisions. Purposefully, we avoid discussions of criteria, guidelines, and thresholds for one-size-fits-all approaches. Rather, as mentioned, we focus our attention on the conceptual and theoretical issues of measurement that are often given minimal attention in existing measurement resources.

TERMINOLOGY

A key challenge in writing this book was selecting terminology and definitions that reflect common usage accurately in the measurement literature. A quick tour of this literature gives rise to many synonyms and definitions. For example, factor analysis is sometimes referred to as *latent-variable modeling, latent-structure analysis*, and *covariance structure analysis*. We encounter words such as *manifest, observed*, and *measured variables*, which have common (and sometimes uncommon) definitions. We find that researchers refer to *variables, concepts*, and *constructs* interchangeably. In this book, we try to sort out some of the inconsistencies, particularly when they have important implications for the research being conducted. We worked in earnest to ensure this book is consistent with contemporary and widely held views in the measurement literature.

PHILOSOPHICAL AND THEORETICAL ORIENTATION

Those of you who are naive to the theory and practice of measurement will not readily discern the philosophical and theoretical debates in the literature. The brevity of a handbook precludes us from identifying and breaking down the various debates. For example, as said earlier, validity is the most important feature of measurement, so it stands to reason that we have clarity on what validity is. We tried to ensure appropriate attention to the philosophical and theoretical camps that guided our writing. We offer a blanket apology for the exclusion of any particular topic that you may consider particularly relevant to your own research agenda.

Many of the arguments in this book are based on practical arguments as opposed to logical arguments. Although logical arguments can be presented in some type of a proof or a mathematical equation, practical arguments are subjective and require various strands of theory and evidence to support a particular position. Our positions and the underlying argument are, for the most part, consistent with or influenced by *Standards for Educational and Psychological Testing* (American Educational Research Association [AERA], American Psychological Association [APA], and National Council on Measurement in Education [NCME], 2014), hereafter referred to as the *Standards*. The *Standards* is prescriptive in nature with respect to constructing and using measures. Its development was carried out jointly by the AERA, the APA, and the NCME. Although these national organizations represent the fields of education and psychology, it is important to recognize that the support received from numerous other professional organizations, credentialing boards, governmental units, test publishers, and academic institutions is extensive. No professional social work organization to date has participated in the development or revision of the *Standards*. This is clearly a mistake, given the heavy emphasis on evidence-based practice.

RELEVANCE OF MEASUREMENT TO QUALITATIVE RESEARCH

It should come as no surprise to suggest that this book was written primarily for the quantitative researcher. The text is certainly not intended to fuel any further divide between qualitative and quantitative research. In fact, we hope the book bridges the two seemingly disparate yet complementary types of research. We do not offer any guidance on what some researchers might refer to as *qualitative measurement*, because we don't believe measurement is possible without the assignment of some numeric value, although in Chapter 2 we do refer to precision at the qualitative level of precision (i.e., categorical and ordinal measurement). At the same time, we believe in the value of qualitative research. With respect to measurement, we believe qualitative research plays very important roles, such as defining the domain space of concepts we seek to measure and generating new hypotheses to promote rigorous tests of measurement theory.

We also believe that an understanding of measurement adds value to qualitative researchers. Many of the problems studied by qualitative social workers imply some type of measurement, particularly in the context of relations between two (or more) variables. For example, whenever we use terms such as *more, less, increasing, decreasing, stronger,* and *weaker,* we are implying some type of relationship between two variables that implies quantitative values, even if we have not created or used a measuring device to document any sort of relational claim. A review of almost any qualitative research study reveals terminology that implies some type of measurement at the categorical or ordinal level. Having an awareness of the fundamental principles of measurement can add precision to qualitative research and provide the necessary bridge to conceptualize and promote the development of measurement to test hypotheses.

2

Foundations and Key Concepts

It was a great step in science when [women and] men became convinced that, in order to understand the nature of things, they must begin by asking, not whether a thing is good or bad, noxious or beneficial, but of what kind it is? And how much is there of it? Quality and Quantity were then first recognised as the primary features to be observed in scientific inquiry.

—James Clerk Maxwell (1870)

WHAT IS MEASUREMENT?

Measurement is the process of assigning numbers to phenomena to represent quantities of attributes. This definition is a modest refinement of the most influential definition of measurement given by Stevens (1946) during the middle of the 20th century: "the assignment of numerals to objects or events according to rules" (p. 677). These definitions imply that measurement is a form of selective description using rules that are consistent with practical or theoretical purposes—meaning, measurement is unavoidable and fundamental to our understanding of the world and how it works. This chapter builds on the basic definition of measurement to provide a thorough discussion of its meaning and uses.

Throughout this book, we use the term *construct* regularly to refer to the theoretically defined "concept, attribute, or variable that is the target of measurement" (Haynes, Richard, & Kubany, 1995, p. 239). Constructs can be thought of as complex concepts (e.g., intelligence, well-being, depression) that are inferred or derived from a set of interrelated attributes (e.g., behaviors, experiences, subjective states, attitudes) of people, objects, or events typically embedded in a theory, and often not directly observable, but measured using multiple indicators.

Thus, constructs are an integral part of the measurement problems we face in social work research. We begin this chapter by highlighting standardized measures. Next, we consider definitions, followed by the kinds of assumptions made in measurement and the levels of precision used. Last, we conclude the chapter with a discussion of the pivotal role played by measurement throughout the research process and theory construction.

STANDARDIZED MEASURES

This book discusses the development and use of standardized measures. Standardized measures refer generally to any type of instrument (e.g., scale, test, inventory) that uses uniform procedures to collect, score, interpret, and report numeric results. They usually haves norms and empirical evidence of reliability and sometimes validity. It is common for standardized measures to be based on multiple items that are aggregated into one or more composite scores, especially when measuring constructs. The procedures used with standardized measures most often include items or indicators, and they can come in many different forms, such as a question designed to measure an ability, a statement to elicit a level of belief, a count of some specific behavior, and so forth.

Standardized measures are recipes that provide specific directions for quantifying phenomena. For example, the Beck Depression Inventory (Beck, Steer, & Carbin, 1988) is one of the more common standardized measures of depression; the CAGE questionnaire is a brief, standardized measure of alcohol use disorders (Mayfield, McLeod, & Hall, 1974); and the Minnesota Multiphasic Personality Inventory

(Graham, 1987) is a standardized personality assessment. These are just a few of the thousands of standardized measures found or referenced in professional journals. Just as cooking recipes allow different cooks to make the same cake, standardized measures allow different researchers to observe the same phenomena. Because the directions are the same for all applications, standardized measures produce data that are considered objective, allowing others to verify the results independently.

In contrast, unstandardized measures lack specific directions governing their use, administration, scoring, and interpretation. Unstandardized measures include open-ended questions, which allow respondents to make interpretations of various concepts and provide responses that do not have any specific rules or fixed formats. Unstandardized measures invite error and confusion, and thus are best avoided by scientists and practitioners alike. Standardized measures are designed to generate detailed and consistent data, giving us the ability to describe phenomena accurately and to create knowledge. Although developing standardized measures can be resource intensive initially, in the long run they are economical. That is, they are used in original research and subsequent studies, and they help to replicate existing research. Indeed, standardized measures are necessary to replicate research findings and thus are fundamental to science, and are critical to evidence-based practice. The overall development of knowledge and the advancement of science depend on standardized measurement.

MEASUREMENT DEFINITIONS

A critical starting point for selecting and using measures, and for developing them, involves defining the measure. Measurement definitions are separated into two different classes: a nominal definition and an operational definition.

Nominal Definition

A nominal definition, also referred to as a *conceptual definition*, involves giving a specific meaning to a construct, usually with synonyms or related concepts, as opposed to the activities or operations used to measure it. The importance of establishing a clear and concise conceptual definition of a focal construct cannot be overemphasized. As MacKenzie (2003) argues, failing to develop a nominal definition produces a series of problems. These problems include barriers to developing measures that represent its domain faithfully and difficulty in specifying how the construct relates to its measures.

It is common for constructs to have different nominal definitions depending on the specific area of study. For example, in addictions research, the construct *recovery* was defined by the Betty Ford Institute Consensus Panel (2007) as "a voluntarily maintained lifestyle characterized by sobriety, personal health, and citizenship" (p. 221). In the area of disaster research, *recovery* has been defined as a set of related activities designed to return a community to a normal level of functioning (Mileti, 1999). These are both nominal definitions of recovery. Other definitions of recovery exist in both the addictions and disaster research areas. Differences in nominal definitions are the result of different assumptions and theoretical orientations brought to bear on the measurement problem.

Constructs that we study often have multiple dimensions or facets. Please note that a construct is a concept implied theoretically from observations, not something observed directly. It is important that these theoretical dimensions be specified and communicated in nominal definitions. Dimensions represent the different ways that phenomena can vary. In other words, they represent a quantitative quality or property (i.e., attribute) of a person, object, or event. Thus, dimensions stand out as the core element in our constructs. The set of items in a measure are unidimensional when the correlations among the items can be accounted for by a single construct or factor that describes the phenomena. The dimensions of a construct are distinct when they represent different aspects or attributes of the construct and thus must be measured separately. These different dimensions are interrelated because each dimension, although distinct, is a part of the same phenomena, as expressed in the nominal definition.

Using the example of recovery from addiction research, three unique dimensions are revealed in the nominal definition: *sobriety, personal health*, and *citizenship*. In general, it is best to use single-dimension measures. Research findings are a direct function of the particular dimensions studied. Sometimes a construct has a very large set of dimensions, making it prohibitive to study all the dimensions at a given time. It is essential that conclusions from research be based on the particular dimensions studied. Stating a conclusion about *recovery* when the measure used was limited to *sobriety* increases the likelihood of adding conflicting or confounding results to the literature. Using single-dimension measures enhances our ability to interpret findings and to communicate results clearly.

It should be noted that the examples of nominal definitions provided earlier are described and clarified in much greater detail in the original sources. Rarely can a single sentence be adequate for providing a nominal definition of a construct.

Operational Definition

Nominal definitions help communicate which constructs are being measured, but not how to measure the constructs. We must go from conceptual to procedural descriptions, indicating exactly what is to be observed, how the observations are to be made, and the assumptions governing these observations. We do this by using operational definitions. Operational definitions describe the specific directions or procedures ("operations") for quantifying a construct. They are the specific activities (or operations) used to measure the construct. There will be as many operational definitions of a construct as there are dimensions to describe it.

Indicators are used to represent operationally the constructs defined in the research question. A construct can be quantified in many different ways, although most often and preferably multiple indicators are used. The use of indicators in social research facilitates accurate communication (Nunnally, 1978). It is important to keep in mind that the indicators are the basis for providing data to produce information, not judgment. Different researchers observing the same phenomena using the same indicators may arrive at different conclusions. Regardless of the researcher's assumptions and interests, the important point here is that the relationships or hypotheses studied are based explicitly on the indicators used.

Continuing the earlier example about addictions research, sobriety is one of the three dimensions of recovery an addiction. An indicator of sobriety is the number of days abstinent from alcohol and all other nonprescribed drugs. *Personal health* and *citizenship* are also separate dimensions of recovery that require separate sets of indicators. The operational definitions are used to create standardized instruments and scales. For example, the Beck Depression Inventory (Beck, Steer, & Brown, 1996) is a standardized scale because it contains a set of indicators (i.e., 21 self-report items) along with specific directions for administering, scoring, and interpreting the results.

Sometimes our measurement problems are deceptively simple, especially when the concepts we use are part of everyday language. Without careful thinking, we can make a host of mistakes that results in errors and biases in our measurements. An example from organizational research illustrates this point. When we talk about the "size" of a social service organization, we may be referring to the number of clients served by the organization. This is a nominal definition because it tells us *what* we are studying. As an operational definition, we could stipulate that organization size refers to the number of clients who have had at least one service contact with the organization during the calendar year.

Based on the nominal and operational definition of organization size, two organizations may be equivalent in size but different in other ways. For example, let's consider the size of two different schools of social work. The number of registered students may be the same, but they could differ on numerous other dimensions, such as total financial capital, ratio of full-time to part-time faculty, annual operating budget, number of courses offered, number of part-time and full-time staff, and number of distinct operating sites. In other words, organizations may be large in one dimension and small in another. This example is important to remember, because it is easy to blur the distinction between our concepts and the phenomena they symbolize. An insight of Zen Buddhism is that all concepts are, necessarily, distortions of reality, but some are more useful than others. Recognizing this helps us minimize the distortion in our research.

The distinction between nominal and operational definitions suggests at least two distinct levels of abstraction: one conceptual and the other empirical. This distinction is important because it represents two different ways of thinking (Blalock, 1968). On the one hand, we form or borrow concepts to symbolize phenomena and their interrelationships. This is the language of theory or conceptual abstraction. On the other hand, we develop empirical indicators, research protocol, and statistical techniques to establish the existence of phenomena and relationships.

This is the language of research or empirical abstraction. Both nominal and operational definitions are required when building scientific knowledge, but the relationship between them is often indirect and complex (Blalock, 1968). We can begin to understand the nature of this complexity by becoming aware of the assumptions underlying measurement and by considering the role of measurement in the process of research and knowledge development.

MEASUREMENT ASSUMPTIONS

Every measurement is based on a set of assumptions. Making these assumptions clear is a difficult and elusive task, in part because there are different kinds of assumptions operating at the same time and in part because it is not possible in any given study to test all the assumptions. Three kinds of assumptions are made: theoretical, procedural, and statistical. Violations of these assumptions almost certainly result in problems with validity, which is our foremost measurement concern. Unfortunately, none of the assumptions have formal tests that help inform whether violations have occurred. It is important to remain cognizant of the various assumptions and to consider each measurement decision carefully in the context of these assumptions.

Theoretical Assumptions

Theoretical assumptions deal with meanings—specifically, the meanings of the qualities represented by the dimensions. For example, two organizations with 100 full-time employees might be assumed to be the same size. This assumption may or may not be sound depending on the type of organizations involved. If both organizations are social service agencies, the assumption might be warranted. On the other hand, if one organization is a social service agency and the other is an automobile manufacturing firm, the assumption is most likely faulty. Theoretical assumptions involve the adequacy of definitions, comprehensiveness and representativeness of the indicators used to represent constructs, variability in the meanings associated with indicators, stability of meaning over time, and many others.

An important theoretical assumption involves specifying the causal relationship between the indicators and the constructs they are intended to represent. In classical measurement theory, it is assumed the indicators of a construct are a reflection of that construct—that is, the indicators are caused by or vary directly as a consequence of the construct. This means the indicators move in unison with the construct. If the phenomena described by the construct increases, then all the indicators of that construct increase. If the construct decreases, all the indicators decrease.

Alternatively, it sometimes makes more sense to think of the construct being caused by or formed through the indicators. For example, in a formative indicator model, stress might be conceptualized as the result of illness, death in the family, job loss, divorce, and so forth. It would not be reasonable to hypothesize that as stress increases these indicators also increase. But, it is reasonable to assume that if any one of these indicators increase, stress increases. The differences, theoretically, between reflective and formative measurement models have important implications. Further discussions of formative and reflective indicators and their relationship with the target construct are included in Chapters 3 and 4, which address validity and reliability. The important point here—and a major theme of this book—is that theory and measurement are interwoven and develop together. One does not get very far without the other.

Procedural Assumptions

Procedural assumptions—often referred to as *operations, operationalizing,* or *operationalization*—underlie the rules of correspondence used in assigning numbers to observations. The importance of these assumptions is noted by Kerlinger (1968), who stated that "no measurement procedure is any better than its rules" (p. 392). Assumptions are made any time we translate observations into categories or degrees of an attribute representing a concept. The procedures specified in an operational definition spell out a set of relations or ordered pairs between the phenomena observed and the numbers used to indicate the range of categories (values) representing the dimension studied. Each unit of observation is assigned a number from the range of possible numbers. Ideally, we want procedures that produce measures that are similar in form to the phenomena being measured. In measurement, this assumption implies the procedure used to assign numbers, so the units of observation are ordered, case-by-case, in the same way they exist in the population. For example, if we measured annual earnings, we would expect the number recorded for the person with the lowest income to have the lowest number recorded, and the person with the highest income would have the highest number recorded. Furthermore, the gradations of numbers from the lowest and highest would be in line with the actual ordering of our sample. Thus, we want the procedures we use to produce measurements that have a one-to-one correspondence to the phenomena being measured.

Statistical Assumptions

Statistical assumptions deal with issues of generalizing from samples to populations. In measurement, there are two distinct uses of statistics for the purposes of generalization. First, when developing measures, we draw samples of content from the *universe of meaning* for a particular concept. For example, we might try to list all the possible ways to observe *burnout, effectiveness,* or *organizational size.* This use of statistics is elaborated through a discussion of the domain sampling model in Chapter 4. Second, when creating knowledge, we sample units of phenomena—behavior, people, organizations—and apply established measures that are summarized using statistics to learn about the population. Every statistic is based on certain assumptions. Many of the statistics used in measurement assume probability sampling. Some statistics make relatively weak assumptions—for example, cases with larger numbers have more of the dimension than those with smaller numbers. Other statistics make more stringent assumptions—for example, the measured values have a normal distribution in the population.

The three kinds of measurement assumptions all deal with information. Theoretical assumptions guide the interpretations given to concepts and the experience or reality that these concepts represent. Usually, more experience with phenomena leads to more information, which in turn increases the precision of description. Procedural assumptions provide bridges between the conceptual and experiential (empirical) worlds. These bridges are strong to the extent that accurate parallels are drawn between the two worlds. Statistical assumptions shape how experience is summarized, and—because the numbers that are summarized represent information (about dimensions of measured variables)—many of the assumptions deal with the amount of information contained in the variables. In other words, the more information we have about phenomena, the more precise we can be in describing them. As you will see, increased levels of precision are achieved in measurement by acquiring additional information.

LEVELS OF PRECISION

The levels of precision in measurement refer to the amount of information available and the relationships between the categories, scores, or values of a variable. Although there are exceptions, qualitative variables have categories and quantitative variables have scores or values. As you might guess, qualitative variables are less precise than quantitative variables. The degree of precision possible depends on how much we know about the phenomena we want to describe. It is useful to recognize that the same concept may be measured qualitatively in one study and quantitatively in another. The variable organizational size, for example, can be measured qualitatively in categories such as "small" or "large," or quantitatively as "the number of members." The distinction between qualitative and quantitative variables can be refined by distinguishing two levels of qualitative variables (i.e., nominal and ordinal) and two levels of quantitative variables (i.e., interval and ratio). These four levels correspond to increasing degrees of precision in measurement. Each level specifies a particular set of assumptions about how precisely the numbers describe the measured attribute. These assumptions, as discussed next, are reflected in the mathematical operations appropriate for each level. Table 2.1 shows how the criteria correspond to the levels of measurement.

Nominal Measurement

Nominal measurement is defined by mutual exclusive and exhaustive classification. The first criteria are mutually exclusive and exhaustive classification. *Mutually exclusive* means that any rating of an object automatically excludes other alternatives. *Exhaustive classification*

Table 2.1 Criteria for Levels of Measurement

Criteria	Qualitative		Quantitative	
	Nominal	Ordinal	Interval	Ratio
Mutually exclusive and exhaustive classification	X	X	X	X
Relative amounts of magnitude/rank order		X	X	X
Standard unit of value			X	X
Meaningful zero value				X

means we have the entire set of categories that defines our concept completely. Nominal measurement is a primitive level of classification and is not to be confused with nominal definitions. Classification is the first and most basic operation in all sciences. When classifying cases, we assign numbers to distinguish different values to the dimension or variable being measured. The purpose is to sort cases into two or more categories that represent differences in important dimensions of the phenomena. For example, we may measure organizational funding base by assigning a 0 value to organizations that are *public* and a value of 1 to those that are *private*. These are mutually exclusive only if the organizations being rated can be classified as either public or private, but not both. They are exhaustive if they contain the full range of possible ratings for that concept—meaning, some type of other organizational funding is not excluded.

The categories for nominal measurement, whether labeled with words or numbers, are simply different. If the dimension is, in fact, important, then the cases in each category will be similar in relation to each other but different from those in the other categories. More important, the pattern of variation represented in the categories will correspond to other variables. Drawing from our previous example, if the "public" and "private" categories are worthwhile, then this measure of funding base will correlate with dimensions of other theoretically justified variables such as turnover, absenteeism, or effectiveness. The *Diagnostic and Statistical Manual of Mental Disorders* of the American Psychiatric Association has relied traditionally on nominal levels of measurement (American Psychiatric Association, 2013). With the exception of the dimensional ratings for personality disorders, all other disorders have criteria for determining whether a given disorder is present or absent in an individual. Thus, when measuring major depressive disorder at the nominal level, use the values 0 and 1 to indicate whether the disorder is absent or present, respectively.

The properties of symmetry and transitivity are assumed in nominal scales. The assumption of symmetry means that if A is judged to be the same as B, then B is the same as A. The assumption of transitivity means that if A is the same as B, and B is the same as C, then A is the same as C. Frequently, as in the example of the funding base, the categories of a nominal classification are assigned numbers: public, 0; private, 1. This is done only to simplify coding and analysis. A researcher could easily replace each number with something else (e.g., 5.002 and 68,088) and achieve the same measurement. It is inappropriate to add, subtract, multiply, or divide nominal categories. Nominal data are summarized by counting the number of cases in each category and controlling for differences in category sizes. The differences in category sizes are usually controlled by calculating proportions and percentages.

Ordinal Measurement

Ordinal measurement is defined by mutual exclusive and exhaustive classification, and by an order representing relative amounts, magnitude, or rank. The relative amounts, magnitude, or rank refer to the qualitative dimensions that allow cases to form an array from low to high, small to large, slow to fast, and so on. Numbers are then assigned according to rank–order position. For example, we could list the size of all organizations in a community and then assign a value of 1 to the smallest, 2 to the next smallest, 3 to the third smallest, and so on, until every organization had a number representing its rank position. Similarly, levels of depression could be rank ordered, where 0 is absent, 1 is mild, 2 is moderate, and 3 is severe.

The usefulness of ordinal scales, such as nominal measurement, depends on how well they relate to other variables. In addition to the assumptions of symmetry and transitivity, ordinal measurement assumes a single continuum underlying the classification or position of cases. The assumption of a continuum is important because it introduces asymmetry between scale values. Thus, although symmetry holds within position values, there is asymmetry between position values. In other words, if organization A is larger than organization B, it cannot be true that organization B is larger than A. The assumption of transitivity is maintained. That is, if organization A is bigger than B, and B is bigger than C, then organization A is bigger than organization C. It is these assumptions of asymmetry and transitivity that justify assigning cases along a single continuum.

Ordinal measurement does not give information on the magnitude of differences between scale values. Knowing that organization A is bigger than organization B does not indicate how much bigger. Similarly, we may know that person A has a more severe form of depression than person B, but we do not know how much more. It is also considered inappropriate to compare a difference between two cases with the difference between two other cases. We cannot add, subtract, multiply, or divide ordinal scale values. It is appropriate, however, to use the mathematical operations of greater than (>) and less than (<) in summarizing ordinal data.

Interval and Ratio Measurement

Interval and ratio measurement are discussed together because almost every interval scale is also a ratio scale. It should be noted that many of the psychological and social concepts that we measure—such as depression, self-esteem, burnout, and group cohesion—do not have standard units. However, through different methods of scaling, we attempt to approximate standard units and treat them as if they are measured at the interval or ratio level of precision.

Interval measurement is defined by mutual exclusive and exhaustive classification, magnitude ordering, and equal intervals between scale values. In contrast to ordinal measurement, interval scales allow us to compare differences between cases based on the attribute. Ordinal rating allows only for a comparison of serial position but not the magnitude of difference. More specifically, assume we have an ordinal rating of annual earnings (measured in dollars) among a sample of 100 persons (1 = low, 100 = high). We can infer that a person with a ranking of 85 has a greater annual earning that somebody with a ranking of 50, but it is impossible to know by how much they are different. The interval or ratio measurement, on the other hand, allows us to calculate the magnitude of difference because the intervals between scale units have a standard unit value—in this case, a dollar.

Ratio measurement is achieved by adding a meaningful zero point to an interval scale. Counting the number of employees as a measure of organizational size is an interval-/ratio-level measurement. Pure interval-level measurement orders cases according to the amount of the dimension, and specifies the exact distance between each case and every other case.

For example, let's assume we have four organizations with a given number of employees: A = 90 employees, B = 80 employees, C = 40 employees, and D = 15 employees. If organizations B and C formed a coalition (B + C), and if organizations A and D (A + D) formed a coalition, the coalition of B and C (80 + 40 = 120) would be larger by 15 members than a coalition of A and D (90 + 15 = 105). In other words, because the distance between scale values is equal, it is reasonable to add and subtract score values. It is also appropriate to multiply an interval scale, even if one of the values is negative; however, it is inappropriate to divide even when both values are positive.

Interval and ratio scales assume a standard unit of measurement that can be replicated. Symmetry and transitivity apply in the same way as noted earlier for ordinal scales. If it is possible to establish standard intervals, however, it is also almost always possible to conceive of a meaningful zero point. This does not mean that there must be an actual case with the value of zero. It means only that the value of zero must make sense for the meaning of the scale. We normally think of an organization with zero employees as no longer existing. Still, this is meaningful on a scale of organizational size, because it defines the end point of the continuum or the absence of organizational size theoretically.

With ratio measurement, we can compare scores by taking their ratios. For example, organization B (with 80 employees) is twice as big as organization C (with its 40 employees [80 ÷ 40 = 2]), and organization A (with 90 employees) is six times bigger than organization D (with 15 employees [90 ÷ 15 = 6]). There is a common misconception that variables such as organizational size do not form a *true* interval or ratio scale, because a difference of 15 employees, for example, has different meanings depending on whether the difference is between sizes of 65 and 50 or between the sizes of 185 and 170. This misconception is really a matter of validity—that is, the inferences from the measurement that are supported by evidence and theory. This measurement example is considered a true ratio scale because we have defined the size of the organization based on the number of people of the organization. Inferences made from the measurements that relate to differential functioning based on the number of employees is a validity argument that must be supported by evidence and theory. In this example, we are not making any inferences from the measurements, only defining the level of precision.

ROLE OF MEASUREMENT IN THE RESEARCH PROCESS

Measurement is often viewed as a particular stage or part of the research process. This view compartmentalizes the various kinds of decisions necessary to carry out research. These decisions include formulating research problems, constructing a design, developing a strategy of data collection, measuring, analyzing, interpreting, and concluding. Models of the research process are typically presented in a serial order. This sequential structure is helpful analytically because it gives the research process a beginning, middle, and end. Usually, the end (conclusions) loops back to the beginning (problem formulation) so that the process, ideally, spirals forward, with each properly executed study helping to build the knowledge base.

A problem with sequential models of research is that the presumed order corresponds only weakly to what researchers actually do. This insightful recognition was made by McGrath et al. (1982), who "regard the research process as a series of logically ordered—though chronologically chaotic—choices" (p. 71). In other words, each stage in the research process has implications for every other stage, and decisions about all stages take place all the time in no particular order. Although this wide-sweeping and crosscutting view complicates our understanding of the research process, it also provides a way to begin dealing with complexity. That is, we must become immersed in the problem areas we study to detect crosscutting interdependencies. This point is consistent with the argument of Mills (1959), who noted that every intellectual craftsperson must be his or her own theorist *and* methodologist. The basis of this argument rests in the complexities of relating nominal and operational definitions. The idea that nominal definitions and operational definitions are related indirectly and reflect different ways of thinking suggests the tremendous intellectual challenge of measurement.

We stimulate our imagination to solve problems by cultivating the ability to shift perspectives between specific observable details and broad general themes (Mills, 1959). In addition, working to understand problems in the context of history and other social forces helps us to make comparisons, derive implications, and find connections where we might not otherwise think to look. The development or use of measures is thus linked inextricably to the development or use of substantive theory. Because this linkage is inherently problematic, the role that measurement plays in the knowledge-building process is now recognized as being pervasive and critical, which suggests the merit of viewing measurement in relation to a complete model of the conceptual stages and empirical techniques that represent the research process (Figure 2.1).

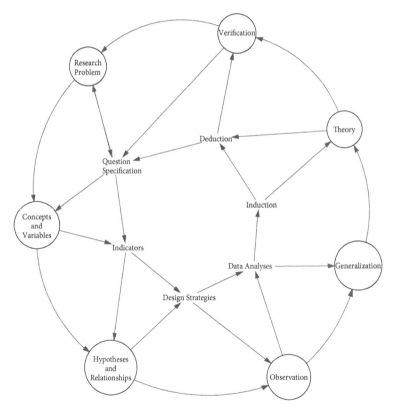

Figure 2.1 The conceptual stages and empirical techniques of the research process.

The model depicted in Figure 2.1 shows conceptual stages as circles around the outer ring of the cycle, and empirical techniques around the inner ring of the cycle. Curved lines indicate connections between conceptual stages; straight lines show links between techniques, and between techniques and conceptual stages. Connections between the conceptual and technical stages correspond to the two distinct languages involved in the research and knowledge-building processes. Although we realize with McGrath et al. (1982) that decisions are made in a "chronologically chaotic" fashion, it helps us to understand the process if we follow the zigzag course of arrows shown in Figure 2.1 between the conceptual and technical stages. As we move from stage to stage, we find measurement implicated in every part of the process. Measurement is implied simultaneously with the conception of a research problem.

TYPES OF RESEARCH

Research problems seek to discover, describe, predict, or explain phenomena. Measurement is often a goal in exploratory studies concerned with discovering new phenomena. The purpose is to gather enough information to raise potentially interesting hypotheses. Descriptive studies are almost synonymous with measurement. Established measures are used to clarify variable distributions. Predictive studies use measures to determine future outcomes. Professional diagnosis is a special case of prediction, because it provides information that governs the course of action. Explanatory studies give reasons for relationships that are predicted. To act on an idea for research, it must be put into words and specified. This specification is accomplished by asking a question.

Exploratory researchers approach a group or situation and ask: Who? What? Where? When? Why? The first fraction of an answer to any of these questions implies measurement. Think about it. Descriptive researchers sample populations to answer questions about how often different categories or scores on a variable or set of variables occur. How many organizations are big? Small? Predictive studies ask: Is it true that X predicts Y? That organizational size predicts burnout? The technique of specifying a question focuses attention on specific concepts and variables, and often on certain dimensions of these variables.

It is impossible to raise a question without including at least one variable. For example, the first question raised by an exploratory researcher about who the actors are in a certain situation contains the concept *actors*. This concept must be defined. As noted in our discussion of nominal definitions, this is a form of selective description that implies measurement. Many of the questions in descriptive research and all questions representing predictions or relationships contain two or more variables. How these variables are defined conceptually determines what can be considered appropriate indicators.

The relationships or hypotheses specified in research questions are understood conceptually from the nominal definitions used to define the concepts, and from the theme or purpose reflected in the research problems. The data collected to describe relationships or test hypotheses, however, derive directly from the indicators, and only indirectly from the concepts and variables, which means important decisions are made on the basis of incomplete information. In other words, unless indicators are perfectly isomorphic with concepts, which is impossible, there is a discrepancy between relationships as conceptualized and as assessed empirically. Here, again, we see how the gap between concept and measure introduces the prospect of error, which leads to design strategies to detect and minimize error.

RESEARCH DESIGN

Research design is, essentially, a plan for generating a consistent, reliable answer to the research question. Every research question implies more than one answer; therefore, it is essential to have a process in place that keeps biases from interfering and instead ensures that we rely on empirical data when formulating our answer.

There are several stages to a research design. The first is the measurement planning stage. During this stage, we evaluate the concepts specified by the research question and determine which indicators can be used to represent those concepts. Then, we choose how to measure those indicators to answer the research question and to rule out alternative answers. It is imperative that the measures we use are as precise as possible, because the more precise the measurements, the less likely that errors are introduced during the observation stage.

The observation stage refers to the actual steps taken to collect data. In an ideal world, we would be able to collect every bit of data we need to formulate a reliable answer, and every bit of data we collect would be unbiased and error free. In reality, human error is certain to influence our observations. There are two basic types of errors that can affect our ability to collect "perfect" data: errors of omission and errors of commission. *Errors of omission* means that necessary data have not been collected. These errors are introduced by subject attrition in experiments, nonrespondents in surveys, and inaccessible or uncooperative informants in exploratory studies. *Errors of commission*, on the other hand, means that the data collected are not necessarily true or would not have been collected if the research design did not include some type of bias. Errors of commission are caused by experimenter bias, the use of leading questions, and the selection of peripheral participants as key informants. Both kinds of errors cause distorted measurement, which can ultimately result in an inaccurate or ambiguous interpretation of the phenomena observed.

Because a certain amount of distortion is inherent in all research, various strategies have been developed to help detect and isolate error during the next stage of research design: data analysis. The purpose of data analysis is to summarize the information collected to formulate an answer to the research question. The first step, summarizing the data, is usually done using tools of statistics. Statistics reduce large amounts of raw data to a manageable form and also aid in making inferences from observational data.

Because the summary process is mostly technical, that part of data analysis is fairly straightforward. The next step, however—the process of interpretation—is where problems arise. Problems of interpretation are very often the result of weak measurement (e.g., measuring attitudes with ambiguous items). For example, if we are assessing satisfaction with a particular service, it is important that we ask questions in a manner that allows respondents to have a uniform understanding of the specific service or aspect of the service that is being assessed. If respondents have different interpretations of what exactly is being assessed, it will be impossible to gather evidence of either validity or reliability, which is the foundation on which to build an accurate interpretation—an issue covered in the chapters on validity (Chapter 3) and reliability (Chapter 4).

Finally, the last stage in a research design is generalization. Generalizations are testable propositions derived in one of two ways: by reasoning from other propositions or by reasoning from empirical evidence. Deductive logic is used to derive propositions from other propositions. Logically valid deductive arguments are those with premises that, if true, provide sufficient grounds for accepting the conclusion as true. This is possible because the premises contain the conclusion, either explicitly or implicitly. Inductive logic, on the other hand, is used to derive propositions from empirical evidence. Valid inductive arguments provide probable but not conclusive grounds for acceptance of the conclusion. This is necessary because inductive logic involves reasoning from what has been observed to what has not yet been observed. It follows that, even with perfect measurement, the truth of the premises does not guarantee the conclusion, because what is true today may not be true tomorrow. Moreover, most generalizations in social science involve statistical inductive generalizations, which means that our knowledge is about probable relations between classes of phenomena, not propositions about specific people or situations.

THEORY

One of the most important take-away messages in this book is that validity is the most important consideration of all measurement issues. Validity refers to the inferences that are supported by theory and empirical evidence. When we refer to theory, we are referring to the sets of interrelated generalizations about certain phenomena, such as a kind of behavior (worker turnover, volunteering, working hard), an attitude (worker burnout, satisfaction, aspirations), a group characteristic (cohesion, conflict, age), or organizational performance (efficiency, effectiveness, adaptability). Theories explain these phenomena by specifying which variables are related and how these relationships work. Understanding such patterns allows predictions to be made. Successful predictions verify the theory. Verified generalizations are impossible without empirical measures. We usually think about the value of a theory as being determined by its empirical support, which ties the value of theory directly to measurement. The more frequent the support (different studies), the more varied the support (different researchers), and the more discriminating the support (quality of studies), the more credible the theory, but also the greater the burden on measurement. If empirical support fails to materialize, theories are supposed to be rejected. Because, however, accurate theories may be evaluated as false for many reasons involving aspects of poor measurement, it is useful to consider developing explicit auxiliary measurement theories along with substantive theories. Our discussion of the research process shows that every part of it depends critically on measurement.

As argued by Nunnally (1978), major advances in science are made possible by breakthroughs in measurement. The conception of a research problem implies certain concepts. Specifying these concepts in a research question focuses attention on particular variables. How these variables get defined conceptually determines the scope of measurement. The choice and construction of indicators sets out exactly what will be studied. Because there is an inherent discrepancy between indicators and the concepts they represent, there is a certain amount of error present in all measurement—that is, the discrepancies between the measured and actual or *true* values of a variable caused by some flaw in the measurement process (which is given considerable attention in Chapter 4). Research designs help to reduce the errors between conceptualization and empirical demonstration. Errors that slip through designs, and those that accumulate from data collection, are estimated in data analysis with statistical techniques. Even with careful implementation of error-reducing techniques, building theory is an uncertain and interminable process. Much of the uncertainty in the research process and in theory building, as we have seen, derives from the gap between conceptualization and measurement. This gap represents the problem of validity—the topic of Chapter 3.

KEY POINTS

- Measurement involves assigning numbers to phenomena to represent quantities of dimensions. Every measure is embedded in a profile of theoretical, procedural, and statistical assumptions. These assumptions deal with how much we know, which determines the precision of our descriptions or measurement.

- We must seek to develop or use standardized measures. Standardized measures generate detailed and consistent findings, facilitate replication of findings, and save resources in the long run.
- Many critical decisions are made on the basis of measurements. The outcomes from these decisions thus depend on the merit of the measures used.
- We must establish clear and concise conceptual definitions of focal constructs by describing what the construct *is* and what it *is not*, by specifying and defining all dimensions of the construct, and by ensuring the items that reflect each dimension are unidimensional and cannot be subdivided into more dimensions.
- Ideas are represented by nominal definitions that name dimensions of phenomena. The empirical world is represented by operational definitions, which specify the procedures for quantifying particular dimensions of phenomena.
- We must specify carefully the relationship between nominal and operational definitions in all measurement problems. This task involves thinking critically about the relationship between our conceptual understanding of a construct (i.e., nominal definition) and the empirical indicators used to measure the construct (i.e., operational definition).
- The combination of four criteria—mutual exclusive and exhaustive classification, relative magnitude, standard unit value, and meaningful zero point—creates four levels of measurement: nominal, ordinal, interval, and ratio. Given a choice, we must always seek the most precise conceptualization possible. Each ascending level of precision provides more information.
- We must work actively toward developing and using measures with the greatest level of precision. Sometimes a lower level of precision may be necessary, such as the measurement of mental or physical disorders. However, we must be cautious of choosing a lower level of precision simply for practical reasons. A clear and comprehensive nominal definition of a construct often reveals at least one dimension that could be measured with a greater degree of precision (e.g., severity).

- We must avoid thinking of measurement as a discrete event embedded within the research process. Rather, think of measurement as the bridge—a critical link—between our substantive theory and empirical techniques.
- We must consider how measurement shapes the development of both theory and methods. All measurement problems should be examined in the context of history and broader social forces.

CLASSIC AND RECOMMENDED READINGS

Blalock, H. M. (1968). The measurement problem: A gap between the languages of theory and research. *Methodology in Social Research*, 5–27.

Kerlinger, F. (1968). *Foundations of behavioral research*. New York: Holt, Rinehart and Winston.

Kuhn, T. S. (1962). *The structure of scientific revolutions*. Chicago: University of Chicago Press.

Mills, C. W. (1959). *The sociological imagination*. New York: Oxford University Press. [Note: This book is considered a classic text for multidisciplinary training in social work research. It provides an essential grounding in social scientific thinking, which is necessary for development of measurement theory.]

Nunnally, J. C., & Bernstein, I. H. (1994). *Psychometric theory* (3rd ed.). New York: McGraw-Hill.

Stevens, S. S. (1946). On the theory of scales of measurement. *Science, 103*, 677–680. [Note: This is a seminal article on the philosophy of operationism. Although the philosophy is no longer widely accepted in the social sciences, the ideas with respect to levels of measurement remain.]

3

Validity

Our clocks do not measure time. . . . Time is defined to be what our clocks measure.

—Anonymous

The quality of measurement is quantified by validity and reliability, and measurements experts universally agree that validity is preeminent (AERA, APA, & NCME, 2014; Hogan & Angello, 2004; Messick, 1989, 1995). A variety of definitions of *validity* can be found in social work literature, with most of them converging on the idea that validity is the extent to which the measure adequately reflects the *real meaning* of the concept under consideration. Validity has then been commonly separated into various *types*—such as construct validity, content validity, convergent and divergent validity, face validity, and factorial validity (see Babbie, 1995). Similar definitions and taxonomies can be found in the social work literature, which we refer to in general as *classical validity theory*. The term *classical* has a variety of meanings (Gillespie, 1988), with definitions that converge on concepts such as "standard," "authoritative," and "traditional." We use the term *classical* in the traditional sense—that is, a system of thought that had significance in earlier times.

The notion that this definition and taxonomy of validity *had significance in earlier times* may come as a surprise to many of you. In fact, a cursory review of measurement papers published in social work journals, especially those using factor analytic methods, shows adherence to classical validity theory based on implicit and explicit definitions of validity, validity-related articles cited, and the manner in which validity is discussed. In our opinion, this adherence has overshadowed significant work during the past two decades to refine and improve our understanding of validity, and this more recent work has basic implications for the type of research we do.

Although important differences exist between classical and modern validity theory, one similarity is worth highlighting: Validity is the foundation of all scientific inquiry. This foundation makes possible the interpretation and use of a measure to support the accuracy of our theories. Without valid measurement, results are meaningless. The purpose of this chapter is twofold. The first is simply to reaffirm the importance of validity theory in social work research. The second is to provide an overview of modern validity theory, highlighting some key differences between it and classical validity theory. This chapter also summarizes the different sources of validity evidence, sources of invalidity, and the process of integrating validity evidence.

The literature on validity theory is vast and complex. It is beyond the scope of this handbook to provide a comprehensive review of this crucial topic. Therefore, we strongly encourage you to familiarize yourself with many of the citations we include to inform and support the various aspects of validity theory described in this chapter. Moreover, the citations as a whole provide a fairly comprehensive summary of certain issues that could not be included.

Modern Validity Theory

Samuel Messick (1989, 1995) has been highly influential in shaping what is now regarded as *modern validity theory*. According to Messick (1989), "[v]alidity is an integrated evaluative judgment of the degree to which empirical evidence and theoretical rationales support the *adequacy* and *appropriateness* of *inferences* and *actions* based on test scores or other modes of assessment" (p. 13, italics in original). Messick's work helped shape the definition of validity presented in the *Standards for*

Educational and Psychological Testing (AERA, APA, NCME, 2014): "the degree to which evidence and theory support the interpretations of test scores entailed by proposed uses of tests" (p. 11).

The definitions of both Messick (1989) and the *Standards* (AERA, APA, NCME, 2014) use the term *test*. In the original sources, both definitions are qualified explicitly so that tests are regarded as any type of evaluative device or measurement. According to the *Standards*,

> [a] test is a device or procedure in which a sample of an examinee's behavior in a specified domain is obtained and subsequently evaluated and scored using a standardized process. Whereas the label *test* is sometimes reserved for instruments on which responses are evaluated for their correctness or quality, and the terms *scale* and *inventory* are used for measures of attitudes, interest, and dispositions, the *Standards* use the single term test to refer to all such evaluative devices. (p. 2; italics in original)

Thus, this general use of the term *test* applies to all measurement instruments in social work research, including but not limited to scales, inventories, ability tests, indices, and process recordings. Again, as noted in the introductory chapter, we use the term *instrument* to refer broadly to the different types of measurement tools used in social work. Our use of this term is congruent with the use of *test* as defined by Messick (1989, 1995) and the *Standards* (AERA, APA, & NCME, 2014).

Although validity is concerned with the interpretation and use of instrument scores, validation is the *process* of collecting data and reviewing theory to support the interpretation of an instrument's particular use. Again, drawing on the *Standards* (AERA, APA, NCME, 2014), "[v]alidation logically begins with an explicit statement of the proposed interpretation of [instrument] scores, along with a rationale for the relevance of the interpretation to the proposed use" (p. 9). Such interpretations involve a detailed description regarding the construct or constructs to be measured, the distinction from other constructs, and the proposed use and interpretation. Because the relationship between a focal construct and other constructs can vary across persons, population groups, settings, and contexts, validation is considered a continuous or ongoing process (Messick, 1995). In a classic paper on construct validity by Cronbach and Meehl (1955), they noted validation involves the same strategies for developing and confirming scientific theories.

What Validity Is Not

Validity is complex, and many of the statements made in social work research lack sufficient precision or make claims that are inconsistent with the modern definition. In fact, we admit to having made such mistakes. For example, a study by Perron, Zeber, Kilbourne, and Bauer (2009) contains a set of examples of the types of problematic statements that are regularly made in social work research:

- "the preliminary findings suggest that the [Health Care Climate Questionnaire] has good face validity, criterion validity, and internal consistency" (p. 575)
- "if shown to be valid . . ." (p. 575)
- "Medication compliance was assessed using the validated Morisky scale" (p. 575)
- "Recent research has shown this scale to have . . . concurrent and predictive validity" (p. 575)
- "The Patient Health Questionnaire-9 has exhibited good . . . convergent/discriminant validity" (p. 576)

These statements are arguably representative of many of the errors pervasive in social work research, especially measurement papers. The purpose in highlighting specific examples is to help make clear that validity theory is vast and complex, and only through the extensive research for this book have the errors of our ways become clear. In this sense, we regard ourselves as reformed sinners and hope that others will follow suit. We carefully selected the words *arguably representative* because we have not examined the research systematically. However, a cursory review of the literature with regard to our claims should make the matter obvious.

The first problem involves statements suggesting that validity is a property of a measure. Although it is typically considered a property in the classical sense, it is not in the modern sense. Validity is the *degree* to which evidence and theory support the *interpretations of a score* derived by a measure (see Messick, 1989). A validity focus is on the interpretation and use of the scores derived by the measure, not on the measurement itself. Thus, using a measure for purposes beyond that supported by the existing validity evidence does not make the measure itself invalid. Any variant of statements such as "this measure is valid" or "this measure has good validity" is misplaced and inconsistent with the modern definition of validity.

The second problem relates to the divisibility of validity, or the separation of validity into different types of validity. In other words, modern validity theory does not break out different *types* of validity such as factorial, convergent, discriminant, construct, content, and so on. Rather, validity is conceptualized as a unitary concept that involves "the integration of any evidence that bears on the interpretation or meaning of the instrument score" (Messick, 1995, p. 742). Therefore, instead of reporting on different *types* of validity, researchers now draw together different *sources of validity evidence*, as described in the following section. This process of integrating threads of evidence from various sources to infer the degree of validity associated with scores or measures of any kind is similar to inductive reasoning. We can now turn our attention to explicating the different sources of validity evidence, which helps to clarify further the important differences between classical and modern validity theory.

Sources of Validity Evidence

When reviewing different sources of validity evidence, we recognize and anticipate some confusion because many of the sources and related procedures for deriving validity evidence can be mapped easily to the classical view of validity theory. But, creating or reading such a map misses the point. From a modern perspective, different sources of validity evidence, as summarized in Table 3.1, all *fuse together* in support of a particular interpretation and use for a measure. Although modern validity theory may appear at first to entail only simple changes in language (e.g., from *types of validity* to *sources of validity evidence*), it will become clear that these changes create a profound shift in perspective. We encourage you to adopt a comprehensive understanding of modern validity theory and apply the new definitions rigorously.

Table 3.1 Sources of Validity Evidence from Modern Validity Theory

Evidence source	Definition	Evidence-gathering strategies
Instrument content	A demonstration that elements of an instrument are relevant to and representative of the target construct	• Conducting a conceptual analysis to establish the logical links between the words and phrases or observations used in an instrument and the construct being measured • Quantifying judgments about the elements of an instrument using formalized scale procedures with multiple experts
Response process	The fit between the construct and the detailed nature of performance or response actually engaged in by examinees (e.g., a measure of self-esteem should not be influenced by social desirability)	• Using think-aloud protocols to understand how individuals are responding to or interpreting items on an instrument • Applying statistical techniques to test for response sets, such as an acquiescence bias
Internal structure	A scaffold that shows the items and subscales exhibit patterns of association consistent with substantive theory	• Using estimates of internal consistency • Conducting formal tests of the factor structure using confirmatory factor analysis
Associations with other variables	The extent to which a measure agrees with another measure of the same construct (criterion evidence) An interpretation of validity on the basis of empirical associations that are expected and the absence of associations that are not expected, which is referred to as *convergent* and *discriminant* (or *divergent*) *evidence*, respectively.	• *Criterion evidence*: Correlating a measure of the focal construct with a criterion that has been measured at the same point in time (concurrent), with a future criterion (predictive) or a previously measured construct (postdictive). A predictive criterion involves correlating a current measure of the focal construct with a future outcome. A postdictive criterion is similar to a predictive criterion, except that it involves use of a previously measured criterion.

	Documentation of the extent to which instrument–criterion evidence can be generalized to a new situation without further study of validity in that new situation (AERA, APA, & NCME, 2014, p. 15).	• *Discriminant convergent evidence:* Testing hypotheses using correlation procedures; summarizing correlations in a Multimethod–Multitrait Matrix (Campbell & Fiske, 1959) • *Generalizability evidence:* Using meta-analytic data to represent the type of situation one is interested in generalizing, because this approach can adjust for statistical artifacts; drawing on the accumulated research to date to make inferences about generalizability
Consequences of measurement	Evaluation of the intended and unintended consequences of instrument score interpretation and use in both the short and long terms	• Documenting the extent to which the intended benefits of a given measure (for a particular purpose) are realized. It should be noted that this type of validity evidence has not been collected or reported routinely since the publication of the *Standards*, which has raised questions about the feasibility and legitimacy of this source of validity evidence.

Note. Table definitions, examples, and strategies are adapted from Messick (1995) and the *Standards* (AERA, APA, NCME, 2015). References cited in the table refer to highly cited articles or articles that provide examples congruent with modern validity theory. The *Standards* (AERA, APA, NCME, 2014) should also be regarded as a suggested (or key) reference for each category.

Those of you who are familiar with classical validity theory will quickly recognize the absence of an evidence source relating to construct validity, because construct validity in general subsumes all forms of validity evidence (see Messick, 1989). In other words, construct validity is validity. Although this aspect of modern validity theory is attributed to the influential works of Messick (1989, 1995), such views first surfaced in the literature about 30 years earlier. For example, Loevinger (1957) argued, "since predictive, concurrent, and content validities are all essentially ad hoc, construct validity is the whole of validity from a scientific point of view" (p. 636).

Content of Measures as a Source of Evidence

Validity evidence from the content of a measure involves demonstrating that the "elements of an assessment instrument are relevant to and representative of the target construct for a particular assessment purpose" (Haynes et al., 1995, p. 239). The content of a measure—that is, the *elements*—includes not only the specific words used to form the items or indicators (questions, statements, perceptions, opinions) of an instrument, but also the formatting of the individual items, response options, and guidelines for administration and scoring (AERA, APA, & NCME, 2014). A clearly specified theoretical domain for the target construct allows indicators to be derived logically. After the indicators are derived, logical and empirical evaluations—also referred to as a *conceptual analysis*—can be conducted to help determine the extent to which the indicators are relevant to the target construct and proposed interpretation of the score. A basic conceptual analysis in support of a validity interpretation can be achieved through the following steps:

Step 1: Examine the conceptual (nominal) definition of the target construct. A construct needs to be defined carefully and unambiguously for items to be derived logically from its theoretical domain. As described by MacKenzie (2003), poor conceptualization leads to problems interpreting item content as evidence supporting validity. When constructing new measures of a construct, a conceptual definition should be subjected to expert review before attempting to generate items presumed to tap the construct.

This recommendation runs contrary to many of the measurement articles published in social work journals. That is, many researchers begin with a pool of items that relates to an imprecisely defined construct. The items are then subjected to an exploratory factor analysis (EFA)—some items are dropped, others may be cross-loaded—but the resulting factor structure produced by the software is used to discover dimensions of the construct or refine its definition, or both. Such applications of factor analysis do not constitute validity evidence. When planning to use an existing measure, it is still important to examine the conceptual definition, and it is essential to examine this definition if the instrument is being considered for a purpose different in any way from the one that guided the measure's creation.

Step 2: Examine each element of the measure in relation to the target construct. It is necessary to evaluate how each element of a measure can influence the results. Begin by considering carefully the relevance, specificity, and clarity of each item in relation to the conceptual definition of the target construct. Next, consider the representation of each item in relation to the construct. When an instrument includes multidimensional constructs, it is imperative that each dimension be examined separately. The elements of each dimension need to be examined, including response format, items, and overall appearance.

Step 3: Quantify judgments using formal scaling procedures. The first two steps of using content to support an interpretation of validity are conceptually driven. Although not common, various quantitative procedures have also been proposed for assessing content to make a validity interpretation. We want to emphasize that quantified judgments cannot replace the essential conceptual evaluations outlined in steps 1 and 2.

Haynes et al. (1995) recommends that every element of the measure be judged by multiple experts using a 5- to 7-point evaluation scale, focusing on relevance, representativeness, specificity, and clarity. Rubio, Berg-Weger, Tebb, Lee, and Rauch (2003) recommend involving both content experts and laypersons. Content experts are professionals with expertise in the field relevant to the measure; laypersons are people for whom the topic of the measure is most salient. These data can be used to formulate what is called a *content validity index* (see Davis, 1992; Rubio et al., 2003), although no guidelines or formal criteria have been given to compute the index or use such an index in making an interpretation of validity. Even in the absence of formal criteria, basic descriptive statistics can provide useful information to help in making informed judgments about each element and the overall measure. We encourage you to review the work of Haynes et al. (1995) for a comprehensive review of the conceptual and empirical procedures involved with using content to establish a validity interpretation for a measure.

Response Processes

Part of building a strong validity argument involves collecting evidence on the responses that reflect differences in actions, strategies, and thought processes of individual respondents (or observers). Differences in responses across respondents (or observers) may be sources of variance that are irrelevant to the construct being measured (Beckman, Cook, & Mandrekar, 2005). For example, a self-esteem measure may evoke a sense of a socially desirable pattern of responses among a subset of individuals. Systematic nonresponse can also be an important source of information about validity—that is, why are some people choosing not to respond to certain items in a systematic way? Our confidence in a measure is compromised when different categories of people reveal differences in their response patterns. Although such differences can result from sampling bias, it is also possible that differences could be the result of something about the measure or measurement process, particularly when asking about sensitive or confidential information. We can produce validity evidence by providing theoretical rationales and data consistent with patterns expected in the measurement process (Messick, 1995).

One method for revealing such variance is the think-aloud protocol. This protocol involves asking participants to explain what they are thinking or how they are interpreting the items contained in an instrument. Responses are coded and then compared among respondents. Think-aloud protocols can be applied to virtually any aspect or kind of measurement; they can be used for specific survey items and survey instructions. Think-aloud protocols can also be used among raters who are doing behavioral observations.

Internal Structure

Internal structure refers to the relationships among items and how these relationships correspond to the theory governing the target construct.

If items are to be combined to form a scale score, it is essential that the total score represent a unidimensional construct. Unless the scale score reflects a single dimension, it would be impossible to establish meaningful associations between variables, to order people based on a specified attribute, to examine individual differences, or to create groups (Hattie, 1985). The unidimensionality of constructs represents one of the most basic assumptions in measurement. Many of the constructs measured in social work research are conceptually complex, meaning that a given construct may contain more than one dimension or conceptually distinct subconstructs (McGrath, 2005).

A unidimensional measure is composed of items that measure the same attribute—ability, achievement, opinion, or attitude—of a specified construct (Hattie, 1985). Unidimensional measures are characterized by item homogeneity. In other words, "homogenous items have but a single common factor among them that are related to the underlying factor . . . in a linear manner" (Green, Lissitz, & Mulaik, 1977, p. 830). Conceptually complex constructs have subconstructs, and each subconstruct is also required to be unidimensional. Streiner and Norman (2008) observed that a construct such as depression "can be thought of as a 'mini theory' to explain the relationships among various behaviors or attitudes" (p. 257). The underlying theory can then provide guidance on how to create summative scores among a set of items representing two or more subconstructs.

Hattie (1985) provides an extensive summary of different methods for examining the dimensionality of a measure, including indices based on response patterns, reliability, principal components and factor analysis, and latent-trait analysis. Each index has its own unique set of strength and weaknesses, but no single index has emerged as a gold standard. Guided by theory, it must be determined that all the items are intercorrelated in a consistent direction. Intercorrelations should be examined using general guidelines suggested by Kline (1979). As a starting point, the range of correlation magnitudes would be from .30 to .70 to ensure some degree of homogeneity while ensuring the coverage is not too broad on the one hand or overly specific on the other. Last, a formal test of dimensionality may involve the use of confirmatory factor analysis (CFA), preferably with tests of other competing model specifications (e.g., a unidimensional model compared with a multidimensional model).

EFA and tests of internal consistency and CFA are commonly used and frequently misused in social work research for gathering evidence on internal structure (Guo et al., 2008). Internal consistency is a statistical procedure to represent the interrelatedness among a set of items, most often summarized using Cronbach's alpha (Cronbach, 1950). Unfortunately, this statistic is often used incorrectly as evidence for establishing item homogeneity or unidimensionality of measure. As argued by Green et al. (1977), a high measure of internal consistency results when a general common factor is present among a set of items. However, it is also possible to obtain a high measure of internal consistency in the absence of a common factor or among a set of heterogeneous items, because measures of internal consistency are influenced positively by the number of items, by the number of conceptually redundant or parallel items, by the number of factors pertaining to each item, and by the magnitudes of the correlations (Hattie, 1985). Items can be correlated for different reasons, only one of which is that each item contained in the overall set of items depends on or is caused by the same underlying construct.

A widely accepted rule in social work research is that the items of a measure should have intercorrelations that yield an adequate estimate of internal consistency, with .70 as the generally accepted cutoff. However, it is prudent to be cautious of such cutoffs because there are important meanings for both low and high interitem correlations. For example, Kline (1979) noted intercorrelations less than .30 suggest that each part of the measure is measuring something different, whereas higher correlations (e.g., .80) may suggest that the measure is too narrow. Cattell (1978) argued that researchers should avoid excessive item homogeneity because it results in bloated factors based on essentially conceptually redundant items, which produces high internal consistency but limits opportunities to gather validity evidence. From this perspective, low to moderate item homogeneity is preferred and helps to ensure that all facets of the construct are being represented. The optimal magnitude of interitem correlation coefficients varies with the scope of the construct or its level of abstraction.

Factor analytic methods are commonly used for acquiring validity evidence related to the internal structure of the measure. From the viewpoint of classical validity theory, this has been referred to as *factorial validity*. EFA can be used to reveal the apparent underlying structure or possible dimensions of a set of variables. EFA is named appropriately because its primary purpose is that of discovery. Such analyses can be useful during the early stages of research to gain new perspectives into the dimensionality of a construct. In other words, it can help researchers identify possible interpretations of data to help sharpen the definition of a construct or inform subsequent validation efforts. However, by itself, EFA, used in an exploratory fashion, does not contribute validity evidence. On the other hand, EFA can be used in a confirmatory manner (e.g., a priori specification of the number of factors implied by the definition or theory, which is subsequently compared with fit statistics after *forcing* the specified number of factors).

CFA is used to test whether a measure of a construct is consistent with the researchers' understanding of the dimensionality of the construct. Researchers specify which set of indicators (measured variables) correspond to which constructs. The specified model is checked to ensure statistical identification, and then is analyzed with data appropriate to the construct to assess model fit. Model fit statistics show the extent to which hypothesized parameters—relationships between each indicator and the latent construct or constructs—are consistent with the data. Besides taking into account measurement error (see Kline, 2012), CFA can be a particularly useful tool in validation efforts by testing competing theories that lead to alternate model formulations (e.g., a single-factor model compared with a two-factor model). Other types of constraints can also be imposed to test the theory further. Consistency between what we expect to find based on theory and what is actually found based on the data provides evidence that, to some degree, supports or fails to support validity interpretations.

Although studies involving CFA typically offer interpretations based on extensive presentations of data, it is imperative that researchers do not underestimate the importance of theory. Model modifications must not occur in the absence of clear theoretical explication. Model modifications can be used to inform our theories, which can then be used to inform revisions to our measures. This is fundamentally different than revising theory to fit a measure, which is not uncommon in social work research. Model modifications can be informative, but any modifications made to the model cannot be tested with the same data because of chance variation present in any sample. In fact, chance variation can be a source of invalidity, particularly in the form of construct-irrelevant variance (reviewed later in this chapter).

Associations with Other Variables

Evidence about the associations of a construct with other constructs is central to establishing its merit relative to a given theory. Three different types of associations are relevant to this form of evidence: instrument–criterion relationships, convergent–divergent evidence, and generalizability.

Instrument–Criterion Relationships

An interpretation of validity can be based on the extent to which a measure agrees with another measure of the same construct. This type of validity is assessed with relational strategies—typically, empirical correlations. In other words, the target construct is correlated with another measure (the *criterion*), and the statistical significance and magnitude of the correlation are the basis for making a validity interpretation. There are three time-based forms of criterion measures: concurrent, predictive, and postdictive. A concurrent criterion involves correlating a measure of the focal construct with a criterion that has been measured at the same point in time (e.g., correlating a worker's self-report of her performance with her supervisor's rating of her performance).

A predictive criterion involves correlating a current measure of the focal construct with a future outcome (e.g., correlating Graduate Record Exam scores with subsequent academic performance). This kind of evidence is collected when we want to use results from a measure (e.g., ACT or SAT) to discern what happens at a later date (e.g., successful graduation from college) to take some course of action in the present (e.g., admit the student to college). This goes back to the central idea of specifying the purpose for which derived scores are to be used.

A postdictive criterion refers to the degree to which the scores from a given measure are related to the scores on another measure that was administered at an earlier point in time, such as using a measure of behavioral misconduct to predict past delinquent acts. This type of validity evidence is not commonly used to support postdictive inferences in many practice situations; however, it is useful for theory building, particularly when testing the relationships prospectively is not feasible.

Making an interpretation of validity on the basis of a criterion has appeal for researchers because it produces a single coefficient that is relatively easy to interpret. However, this appeal has to be considered in the context of its limitations. First, the inference of validity rests fundamentally on the validity evidence linked to the criterion measure. In addition, many of the constructs we study, particularly latent constructs (e.g., self-esteem, social capital, anxiety) lack good criterion measures. Criterion measures are derived from theory and must be selected carefully and studied over time by different researchers using different samples and methods.

The constructs we study in social work research tend to be associated weakly or modestly with other constructs. This state of affairs probably results in part from the dynamic complexity of the situations and phenomena studied, from poor theoretical specification, from the use of measures that have not benefited from any kind of validity study, from the use of measures with weak or inappropriate reliability (e.g., Likert scales of multiple items that have not had their presumed unidimensionality substantiated through factor analysis), from poorly designed studies (e.g., not assessing statistical power or using crude proxies such as "10 cases for each variable" to estimate power), and from using convenience or otherwise unrepresentative samples. We have the ability to improve significantly (and importantly) five of these six limitations.

Convergent and Discriminant Evidence
Making an interpretation of validity on the basis of empirical associations that are expected and the absence of associations that are not expected is referred to as *convergent* and *discriminant* (or *divergent*) *evidence*, respectively. Sometimes convergent and discriminant evidence is described confusingly as similar to a validity interpretation based on a criterion. This is a mistake. Although the procedure of using correlation methods are the same, an interpretation based on convergent or discriminant evidence is distinct from an interpretation based on a criterion because of fundamental conceptual differences. An interpretation of validity based on convergent and discriminant evidence refers to the extent to which *other* theoretically hypothesized measures are or are not related to the focal construct in the expected pattern of associations. As noted earlier, an interpretation of validity based on a criterion refers to the extent to which a measure correlates with an alternative measure of the same construct.

The use of convergent and discriminant forms of evidence is essential to a strong validity interpretation because the performance of a measure is potentially affected by the particular combination of variables comprising the theory. For example, a measure of self-esteem should be related to self-efficacy. The relationship should be high, but not too high; otherwise, the measures could be interpreted as tapping the same construct. The strength of the association might be hypothesized to be .6 or .7 for convergent evidence. A measure of self-esteem may be expected to be unrelated to enrollment in public or private schools. Therefore, to establish discriminant evidence, we might hypothesize the absence of any association between self-esteem and enrollment in public or private schools. The theory that includes the focal construct should inform the selection of convergent and discriminant measures, directions of association, and the strength of associations.

A major advancement in validation procedures involved the Multitrait–Multimethod Matrix (MTMM) developed by Campbell and Fiske (1959). The MTMM was used to examine convergent and discriminant forms of evidence as a practical way to build evidence for a construct's validity. Campbell and Fiske (1959) argued that both convergent and discriminant forms of evidence are necessary but not sufficient conditions for construct validity evidence, which is a view held among modern validity theorists. The MTMM involves measuring several concepts or *traits* using different *methods* (e.g., self-report, behavioral observation). Correlations among the concepts are calculated and then these correlations are arranged in a particular format to facilitate comparisons. Three different types of correlations are easily identified based on their position within the matrix—diagonals, triangles, and blocks. These correlations provide the basis for making reliability and validity inferences. One especially important advantage of the MTMM is the formal, but incomplete, assessment of methods factors. That is, measuring different concepts with the same method (e.g., self-report) can result in inflated correlations among the concept that may be the result of a shared method factor, as opposed to the correlation being attributed to a trait only. This is particularly important to social work research, given that much of social work research is grounded heavily in self-report. The use of the MTMM in social work and other areas of research is not common. The primary reason for this is that it is not always feasible to measure different concepts with different methods (although doing so can result in potentially significant gains in knowledge). The original article by Campbell and Fiske (1959) provides a detailed description of the approach to explicate further the implementation of it and the importance of systematic investigation of convergent and discriminant evidence.

Validity Generalization

Validity generalization refers to "the extent to which evidence of validity based on instrument–criterion relationships can be generalized to a new situation without further study of validity in that new situation" (AREA, APA, & NCME, 2014, p. 18). Issues of generalizability relate not only to population groups and settings, but also to instrument–criterion relationships (see Messick, 1995). Validity generalizations are informed by the accumulation of evidence and review of theory to support the use of an instrument for a given purpose in a particular situation. As indicated in the *Standards,* the accumulated evidence for validity generalization may reveal a need to refine or revise the construct further, or to reveal a need for a certain type of research. Meta-analytic evidence can be used to support or inform validity generalizations because it can summarize important instrument–criterion relationships for different situations.

Consequences of Measurement

Validity evidence derived from the consequences of measurement is arguably the least understood and developed area in modern validity theory. Consequences of measurement refers to the evidence and rationales for evaluating both the intended and unintended consequences of score interpretation, and use in both the short and long terms. For example, in a study of emergency response organizations, findings unexpectedly indicated several organizations without any members. Initially this was thought to be impossible and thus most likely a coding error. A careful review of the data confirmed the number of members as zero for several organizations. A follow-up study discovered these particular organizations existed only to mobilize in the event of a disaster. Therefore, during normal times, they existed as empty shells; but, when a disaster struck, certain designated people immediately assumed roles within these response organizations. The unintended consequence of zero members served to expand and clarify our understanding of how the community responded to disaster. This form of validity is most controversial (see Brennan, 2006; Kane, 2001) because it is unclear how the role of consequences fits within the modern understanding of validity. A systematic review of educational and psychological instruments revealed that consequences of testing as a form of validity evidence "is essentially nonexistent in the professional literature and applied measurement and policy work" (Cizek, Bowen, & Church, 2010, p. 732). We leave it up to you to decide whether a systematic review of a sample of more than 2,400 articles from applied measurement and testing policy journals for the past 10 years is sufficient support for this critical statement about modern validity theory (Cizek et al., 2010; see also Cizek, Rosenberg, & Koons, 2008). We think it is.

SOURCES OF INVALIDITY

Sources of invalidity are arranged in two classes: construct underrepresentation and construct-irrelevant variance (Messick, 1995). Construct underrepresentation, according to Messick (1995), occurs when a measure of a particular concept is "too narrow or fails to include important dimensions or facets of the construct" (p. 742). Construct-irrelevant variance occurs when a measure is too broad and includes reliable excess variance associated with other distinct constructs (Messick, 1995). Construct-irrelevant variance also includes method effects such as response sets or guessing propensities, which are unrelated to the construct being measured. In the measurement of task performance, construct-irrelevant variance can be broken down further into construct-irrelevant difficulty and construct-irrelevant easiness. Surprisingly, social work researchers have remained largely unconcerned with issues related to task performance (e.g., therapy skills, expert knowledge) and, therefore, we refer you to the work of Messick (1989, 1995) and Embretson (1983) for a detailed discussion of construct-irrelevant difficulty and easiness.

The techniques described for deriving validity evidence are the same techniques for identifying sources of invalidity. For example, efforts to derive content evidence may be carried out with a comprehensive conceptual analysis of the measure. This analysis may yield data that do not lend support to validity interpretations. In this case, the conceptual analysis may suggest that the construct being measured does not include an important dimension of the construct (i.e., construct underrepresentation), or that it may be too broad and not distinguishable from other related but conceptually different constructs (i.e., construct-irrelevant variance).

As another example, it is not uncommon for factor analytic studies to suggest two distinct factors among a set of positively and negatively phrased items from a psychosocial rating scale (e.g., self-esteem), with each factor containing either all the positively or all the negatively phrased items (Marsh, 1996). Such analyses can speak to issues of validity with respect to internal structure and response processes. Identifying an acquiescence bias would become evidence for invalidity. Modification indices that are provided by structural equation modeling (SEM) software applications (e.g., LISREL, Amos, Mplus) indicate possible model improvements by allowing error terms to be correlated. High correlations among error terms may be the result in something in common other than the latent construct being measured (e.g., response bias) or even very similar wording.

One must be skeptical and cautious of relying on statistical output for resolving issues of validity. Statistical software packages are completely naive of validity, and we are absolutely confident that no future software release will have a validity add-on. The output from statistical software can, at best, provide clues for potential problems or solutions, and any interpretation must be made in the context of validity theory. Thus, using statistical output to inform changes to a measure without full consideration of validity—such as allowing correlated error terms to be correlated, dropping items, revising items, and so forth—without a strong and explicit substantive rationale, will pollute and sooner or later undermine the process of validity evidence.

INTEGRATION OF VALIDITY EVIDENCE

Validity Arguments

Arguments of validity involve drawing on various strands of research and theory that are organized around an explicit interpretation and use of a given score derived from a particular instrument. This integration is necessary to provide an evaluative summary for validity interpretations. Again, arguments directed toward the "validity of a measure" are misguided. Unfortunately, no formula or explicit method exists on how this integration is to be done. It is simply impossible to apply any sort of weighting system to the various sources of evidence, with the goal of crossing a minimum threshold to establish validity.

Arguments of validity should not be made in a manner that suggests implicitly or explicitly that it is present or absent. Rather, validity is a matter of degree; it will always be imprecise because it cannot be standardized. But, making a validity argument is a necessary part of validation. You will know by the end of this book that unstandardized processes are a primary source of variability.

Potential for Bias

One obvious challenge to making a validity argument is in circumstances when the arguments are made by the developer of an instrument. A lot of time and resources are invested into the development of instrument. Combine this with the ongoing pressures to publish and the well-documented publication bias for positive findings in the scientific literature. These are near-ideal conditions for researchers to make validity arguments that may be tainted by a confirmation bias—that is, look for or interpret evidence to support one's beliefs or hopes and discount refuting evidence.

Although more difficult to handle, negative findings can and should be published. One strategy is to consider the knowledge contributions for both negative and positive findings during the planning stages of a study. The knowledge contribution of positive findings is fairly straightforward, especially when it comes to instrument development. However, negative findings can also be very useful. More specifically, all instruments—without exception—should be guided by theory. Although statistical models are used for generating validity evidence, it is important to remain cognizant that such analyses are sources of evidence relative to a theory. Thus, if an instrument does not perform as expected in a given set of analyses, one must consider the potential sources of the problem. On one hand, this may be the result of technical problems (e.g., instructions that are unclear or ambiguous) or conceptual problems with the instrument (e.g., clear specification of the construct domain).

Alternatively, the theory that guided the development of the instrument could be problematic. In this case, negative findings can (and should) be used to inform modifications to underlying theory. However, using negative findings to inform modifications to underlying theory is much more difficult if the study is conducted with the assumption that the underlying theory is specified correctly.

Role of Statistics

A variety of important resources exist for learning about the methods of demonstrating validity. A number of useful resources are cited in this handbook, and other full-length texts are available to guide validation efforts. Despite the existence of such resources and the preeminence of validity in measurement, it is unfortunate that far more attention is given to reliability (covered in Chapter 4) than validity. For example, Hogan and Agnello (2004) reviewed a sample of 696 measurement-related research reports listed in the American Psychological Association's *Directory of Unpublished Experimental Mental Measures.* They found only 55% of the reports included any type of validity evidence, which was far less than those reporting reliability information. In fact, almost all the articles (i.e., 94%) included some type reliability analysis (Hogan, Benjamin, & Brezinski, 2000a, 2000b). These results may not generalize to the published reports in social work research journals. In fact, most of the measurement-related articles published in social work journals include evidence derived from factor analysis. However, it is uncommon to find too much measurement-related research in social work that extends beyond the use of factor analysis. Equally problematic is the general absence of study replications, especially in the context of factor analysis, which may involve capitalizing on chance correlations.

This phenomenon may be the result of an artifact in software advances rather than the actual knowledge contribution to social work research. Also, it is arguably easier to collect and interpret reliability data in comparison with the full range of validity-related data to make comprehensive statements about the validity of an interpretation. Some journals only consider reviewing empirical papers, which limits further the opportunity to publish crucial theoretical work critical to the development of measures. This said, notable barriers exist in conducting empirical research to advance our knowledge of measurement validity.

However, the value of social work research is considered worthy only to the extent to which we can make strong arguments for the validity of our uses and interpretations of our measures. Statistics are important, although we may be overreliant on the use of factor analytic methods (and other latent-variable procedures) and may underemphasize the value of using multiple methods and engaging in much-needed theoretical activities.

KEY POINTS

- Validity is the most crucial aspect of measurement. Measurement-related decisions must be considered in the context of validity.
- Significant advances have been made in validity theory during the past 30 years. What one has learned or is currently learning in graduate school may not be consistent with modern validity theory.
- A modern definition of validity is "the degree to which evidence and theory support the interpretations of test scores entailed by proposed uses of tests" (AERA, APA, & NCME, 2014, p. 11). "Test scores" and "tests" refer broadly to all the various types of instruments used in social work research.
- Validation is the process of collecting data and reviewing theory in support of interpretation of use. It is an ongoing process that involves the same techniques and procedures used in theory testing.
- Validity is not a property of the measure. It is a property of the interpretation of the score produced by the measure.
- Validity is not divisible into different types. Validity is a unitary concept, and interpretations of a score need to be supported by different sources of validity evidence.
- Sources of validity evidence include instrument content, response process, internal structure, relations to other variables, and consequences of measurement.
- Sources of invalidity include construct underrepresentation and construct-irrelevant variance.

- Validity arguments require an explication of the theory of the measure along with an integration of the validity evidence to justify score interpretations and use.
- Arguments regarding the validity of score interpretation should be stated in terms of *degree*, not in terms of whether validity exists.
- Statistics per se are irrelevant to validity and can be misleading in the absence of strong theory.

CLASSIC AND RECOMMENDED READINGS

American Educational Research Association, American Psychological Association, and National Council on Measurement in Education. (2014). *Standards for educational and psychological testing.* Washington, DC: American Educational Research Association.

Bollen, K., & Lennox, R. (1991). Conventional wisdom on measurement: A structural equation perspective. *Psychological Bulletin, 110*(2), 305–314.

Borsboom, D. (2008). Latent variable theory. *Measurement, 6,* 25–53. [Note: Although modern validity theory has widespread acceptance (among those who are familiar with both classical and modern validity theory), it is important to recognize thoughtful critiques and alternative views. We encourage you to consider some other views that challenge some of the core tenets of modern validity theory. This article is an excellent point of departure.]

Borsboom, D., Mellenbergh, G. J., & Heerden, J. V. (2004). The concept of validity. *Psychological Review, 111*(4), 1061 1071.

Campbell, D. T., & Fiske, D. W. (1959). Convergent and discriminant validation by the Multitrait–Multimethod Matrix. *Psychological Bulletin, 56,* 81–105. [Note: Campbell and Fiske introduce the concept of the MTMM, which helped overcome methodological and substantive problems associated with convergent and discriminant relationship studies in validation efforts. Although this article was written during and consistent with the language of classical validity theory, the content remains highly relevant for understanding issues of convergent and discriminant evidence in the context of common method variance.]

Cizek, G., Bowen, D., & Church, K. (2010). Sources of validity evidence for educational and psychological tests: A follow-up study. *Educational and Psychological Measurement, 70*(5), 732–743.

Cronbach, L. J., & Meehl, P. (1955). Construct validity in psychological tests. *Psychological Bulletin, 52,* 281–302. [Note: This article introduced the concept of construct validity and is now considered a classic measurement article. Although some of the ideas are not discussed regularly in empirical social work literature, they remain useful in helping clarify our understanding of constructs we want to measure. One such idea is what they call the *nomological net.*]

Embretson, S. (1983). Construct validity: Construct representation versus nomothetic span. *Psychological Bulletin, 93*(1), 179–197.

Hattie, J. (1985). Methodology review: Assessing unidimensionality of tests and items. *Applied Psychological Measurement, 9,* 139–164. [Note: This is a very comprehensive article that provides a detailed review of the different methods for assessing the internal structure of an instrument, with an emphasis on establishing unidimensionality.]

Haynes, S. N., Richard, D., & Kubany, E. S. (1995). Content validity in psychological assessment: A functional approach to concepts and methods. *Psychological Assessment, 7*(3), 238–247.

Kane, M. T. (2006). Validation. In R. L. Brennan (Ed.), *Educational measurement* (4th ed., pp. 17–64). Westport, CT: Praeger.

Loevinger, J. (1957). Objective tests as instruments of psychological theory. *Psychological Reports, 3,* 635–694.

McGrath, R. (2005). Conceptual complexity and construct validity. *Journal of Personality Assessment, 85*(2), 112–124.

Messick, S. (1989). Validity. In R. L. Linn (Ed.), *Educational measurement* (3rd ed., pp. 13–103). New York: Macmillan.

Messick, S. (1995). Validity of psychological assessment: Validation of inferences from persons' responses and performances as scientific inquiry into score meaning. *American Psychologist, 50*(9), 741.

4

Reliability and Measurement Error

Although this may seem a paradox, all exact science is dominated by the idea of approximation. When a [person] tells you that he knows the exact truth about anything, you are safe in inferring that he is an inexact [person]. Every careful measurement in science is always given with the probable error . . . every observer admits that [she or] he is likely wrong, and knows about how much wrong [she or] he is likely to be.

—Bertrand Russel (2001)

CLASSICAL TEST THEORY

Reliability is the degree to which measurements are free from error, making reliability inversely related to error (Barman, 2011). The *Standards* defines reliability as "the consistency of the scores across instances of the testing procedure" (AERA, APA, & NCME, 2014; p. 33). Reliability goes *hand-in-hand* with validity; any reputable introductory research methods book will emphasize that reliability is a condition for validity. The amount of literature on the topic of reliability is further suggestive of its importance because the amount of this literature dwarfs that of validity. Unfortunately, this may give the impression that reliability shares the same importance as validity, which is incorrect and potentially harmful. Reliability is a necessary *but not sufficient* condition for validity. Reliability can exist without validity but validity cannot exist without reliability. This point is elaborated later in this chapter, but keep in mind that the paramount issue in measurement is validity. The attention given to reliability is likely a result of the fact that it is more amenable to quantification than validity. Reliability is very important and a necessary condition for assembling the evidence to support an interpretation of validity. It is critical that reliability be considered in the context of validity.

Reliability and measurement error mirror each other. Understanding reliability requires understanding measurement error. In this chapter, we first introduce the concept of measurement error from the perspective of classical test theory (CTT). The focus is on CTT because it serves as the foundation of reliability in social work research. Our introduction presents the fundamental equation of CTT. Next, we provide an overview of the model and the various types and sources of measurement error. Then, we review different methods for assessing reliability. We conclude this chapter by briefly describing two other models—G-theory and IRT—that are used to conceptualize and evaluate measurement error.

CTT dominates the measurement literature for the purposes of understanding and estimating measurement error. It has appeal because of its simplicity, although some consider this problematic because they believe it oversimplifies the complexity of measurement error (Brennan, 2000). From the perspective of CTT, a measurement has two parts. The first part is the error-free *true score*, denoted by T. This is an expected value or hypothetical average score based on many trials of a measure or administrations of a measurement device (e.g., scale). The observed values denoted by X are used to estimate the true score. The difference between the observed values and the true scores are the errors of measurement, denoted by E. These relationships are summarized in what is called the *fundamental equation*: $X = T + E$. That is, a measurement is equal to the true score plus the measurement error.

DOMAIN-SAMPLING MODEL

According to Nunnally and Bernstein (1994), "the most useful model of measurement error considers any particular measure to be composed of responses to a random sample of items from a hypothetical domain of items" (p. 216). Sometimes the *domain* is referred to as a *universe* or *population* of items because it assumes that all items or variables indicative of the concept being measured are included. Nunnally and Bernstein (1994) appropriately prefer the term *domain* to avoid confusion with other sampling-related practices such as sampling persons from a population. It is helpful to think of this domain as a matrix, because the model involves correlating each item with every other item in the domain.

We describe the domain-sampling model with an example of measuring attitudes toward evidence-based practice. Think about a measure of attitudes designed to describe all aspects of evidence-based practice. The domain of such a measure would include a statement or item that represents every conceivable aspect of evidence-based practice. The number of such items would be very large. A person's true attitude toward evidence-based practice would be obtained by having that person respond to all items in the domain. Of course, it is evident—given the size of the domain—that constructing and administering such a measure is not feasible. Fortunately, the domain-sampling model establishes the foundation for drawing reliable measures.

The model assumes an infinite pool of items but works well with large samples of items. A domain of 100 items would yield results very close to those derived by assuming an infinite number of items. A person's attitude on each aspect would be correlated with every other aspect in the domain. Naturally these individual correlations would vary, because each item is unique to some degree and also contains some error. However, each item also shares with every other item a common relation to attitudes regarding evidence-based practice. These relations are assumed to be of equal strength. In other words, each item contributes equally to the common core of attitudes toward evidence-based practice. This common core of measured content is reflected in item averages calculated across the domain.

The average correlation of each attitude item with all the others in the domain is the same. That is, the average correlation value of each column in the domain is the same. This happens because all items (aspects of evidence-based practice) are weighted the same. Keep in mind that it is the average for each variable that is the same; the individual item correlations vary. In addition, the average correlations at the base of each column are also the same as the average overall correlation of all items in the domain. This overall correlation indicates the common core of attitudes toward evidence-based practice. This common core is not necessarily a single factor. For example, a person's attitude toward aspects of direct client relations may be different than her attitude toward aspects of the paperwork associated with evidence-based practice. The range of correlations in this domain shows the amount of variance that exists in attitudes toward evidence-based practice.

An expansion of the formula used to correlate one variable with the sum of a set of variables is used to calculate the average correlation of each item with all others in the domain. Nunnally and Bernstein (1994) provide a detailed illustration of this calculation using standardized scores. By convention, the correlation of one item or a set of items with another item or set of items yields the *reliability coefficient* of that item or set of items. In addition, the square root of the reliability coefficient equals the correlation of that item with the domain *true* score. This correlation can be treated like any other in the equations for correlation analysis. Because squaring a correlation gives the variance accounted for in one variable by another, squaring this correlation with the *true* score is equal to the percentage of explained true score variance. These calculations reveal that the reliability coefficient equals the amount of true score variance divided by the actual variance of the measure. This model of reliability sets the stage for many principles concerning measurement error.

The domain-sampling model reveals that the average correlation of one attitude item with a sample of the others from the same domain would provide an estimate of that item's reliability, and the square root would estimate the correlation with the hypothetical true score of attitude toward evidence-based practice. A measure created from a sample of items is reliable to the extent that it correlates highly with the true score. The more items included in the measure, the more reliable the measure. Of course, reliability increases with the additional items only if the items are unique and are selected randomly from the domain-sampling model. In practice, we can only, theoretically, derive items from the domain-sampling model, so making measures longer does carry important risks, such as conceptual drift and redundancy.

The domain-sampling model also suggests that we can easily construct multiple versions of the same measure by selecting sets of items randomly from the domain. Again, in practice, this is not necessarily that straightforward, because we cannot sample randomly from the domain. Construction of multiple versions would require a large set of items that are unique, nonredundant, and highly correlated with the true score. A large set of items would provide a basis for constructing multiple versions of the same measure, but it is unlikely that the multiple versions are ever exactly the same.

Our description of the domain-sampling model raises two issues that deserve careful consideration. It is helpful to remember that the domain-sampling model is a theoretical model that we can approximate only in practice. The distinction is reflected in Figure 4.1. The theoretical model is infinitely large and covers all facets of the domain. Thus, if items in the domain could be represented graphically with the letter *i*, the domain is entirely covered. However, from a practical standpoint, the domain is finite. This is not a serious problem, assuming that the actual domain of items is large relative to the scope of the concept. Some conceptual domains are very large, such as the example with attitudes toward evidence-based practice. Concepts defined more narrowly, such

Theoretical

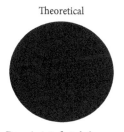

Practical

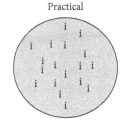

• Domain is infinitely large
• Contains all possible items
• Items are randomly selected

• Domain is very large, but finite
• Items are constructed
• Items are purposively or randomly
  selected from set of constructed items

Figure 4.1 Graphical representation of the domain-sampling model.

as attitudes toward a specific policy or single facet of practice, have smaller domains.

The second issue relates to the random selection of items from the domain. From a theoretical standpoint, we would have a sampling frame and strategy that would allow us to select randomly from this domain. In practice, however, we almost always construct items that we think represent particular facets of the domain. Again, this is not a serious problem if we have a clearly defined concept that informs the construction of items. When creating a measure, we want the largest pool of items possible to ensure all facets of the concept are represented. Even so, it is often not feasible to create a pool of items that allows for random sampling. Typically, measures are created purposefully to represent the defined meaning of a concept.

Although the domain-sampling model is helpful in understanding measurement error, it is perhaps even more critical to issues of validity. Whether researchers are creating new items or using existing items, they must remain cognizant of the underlying theory used to define the domain. For example, in the context of true score or latent-variable models, researchers must be clear about how the measurement items relate to the latent variable. That is, some items may define the target construct, whereas others may reflect the construct. (This issue is elaborated further in Chapter 5.) Failure to make this theoretical distinction may not be evident when we assess reliability, but it will create serious complications with respect to validity.

RANDOM AND SYSTEMATIC ERROR

Two types of measurement error—random and systematic—are differentiated in CTT. Random error is a class of errors that is not correlated with the construct, other measures, or anything else under study. Random errors distribute symmetrically around the true value, with some observed scores being greater than the true score and others being less than the true score. These errors balance each other out, making the expected value (mean score) the best estimate of the true score. However, this should not suggest that random error is not problematic. In fact, much of social work research involves relating variables with each other—and random error results in distortions of almost all statistics that social work researchers use.

We can use self-reported behavior as an example of random errors. The measurement error would be considered random if the respondent's mistakes in reporting a given behavior were the result of fatigue, forgetfulness, illness, inaccurate guessing, or any kind of unintentional underestimate or overestimate. With random error, the assumption is that all the factors contributing to the variability are random and, therefore, balance each other out. An interesting consequence of random errors is that they attenuate or decrease the correlation between two variables. However, random errors are more problematic in multivariate models.

Systematic error exists when measures concentrate around alternative values instead of the true value. In other words, the observed scores are not distributed symmetrically around the true score; instead, they are biased consistently upward or downward. This means that the errors do not balance each other and the mean value over- or underestimates the true value.

Systematic error can arise from any part of the system we are studying. Following the previous example, a systematic error may be present when respondents under- or overreport behaviors intentionally as a result of social desirability. For example, in a study of healthy behaviors, the respondent may feel inclined to overreport healthy behaviors (e.g., amount of exercise) and underreport unhealthy behaviors (e.g., cigarette smoking). Systematic error affects the intercept but not the magnitude of the correlation coefficient.

The distinction between random and systematic error is crucial. In our CTT models of measurement error, we are assuming error to be random. Although CTT does not consider systematic error, this type of error can affect the reliability of scores and, worse, can distort validity. In practice, the distinction between random and systematic error is not always clear, and "[s]ources of error associated with random error can sometimes lead to systematic error" (Viswanathan, 2005, p. 143). Before discussing particular sources of measurement error, we take a closer look at the consequences of measurement error.

CONSEQUENCES OF MEASUREMENT ERROR

As noted at the outset of this chapter, reliability is a *necessary but not sufficient condition* for validity. The consequences of measurement error are rather straightforward: "Random error of measurement distorts virtually every statistic computed in modern studies. Accurate scientific estimation requires correction for these distortion in all cases" (Schmidt & Hunter, 1996, p. 200). The significance of measurement error is often underappreciated among researchers. This is evident with the issue of arbitrary thresholds in reliability assessment. For example, many researchers believe that Cronbach's alpha (an estimate of reliability discussed in the following section) is acceptable at a level of .70 or higher. And it is not uncommon to find research articles reporting measures with even lower levels of reliability, along with arguments that the measures are approaching this critical threshold.

Table 4.1 helps reveal the arbitrary nature of the threshold approach to reliability. In addition, this approach is especially problematic when we are using numerous measures with low levels of reliability. More specifically, this table (adapted from Schmidt and Hunter [1999]) shows the influence of measurement error on the average correlation between two constructs X and Y. Assume we know that the zero-order correlation between two constructs is .50. We can see how the reliability of the measures affects the correlations between the two variables. With reliabilities close to 1.0, the observed correlations are close to the known true correlation. For example, when measures of X and Y have estimated reliabilities of .90, the attenuation of the correlation is .45 compared with the actual correlation of .50.

Researchers who take a relaxed view with respect to reliability, allowing estimates at or below this arbitrary cutoff, produce results that are

Table 4.1 Influence of Measurement Error on Average Correlation between Y and X When the Actual Correlation Is .50

Reliability of measure Y	Reliability of measure X					
	.40	.50	.60	.70	.80	.90
.40	.20					
.50	.22	.25				
.60	.25	.27	.30			
.70	.27	.30	.32	.35		
.80	.28	.32	.35	.37	.40	
.90	.30	.34	.37	.40	.42	.45

Note: Adapted from Schmidt and Hunter (1999, p. 186).

inconsistent, distorted, and difficult to interpret. When the estimates of reliability for both X and Y are .70, we underestimate the strength of the relationship by 30% below its correct value (Schmidt & Hunter, 1996). The following equation—in other words, the single correction—yields a correction for the unreliability in the criterion variable (y), not the test variable (x) (Muchinsky, 1996), which is the most common procedure for the correction of attenuation. In this equation, ρ_{xy} represents the corrected validity coefficient (i.e., correlation between the test [x] and the criterion [y] variables), r_{xy} is the observed validity coefficient, and r_{yy} is the reliability of the criterion:

$$\rho_{xy} = \frac{r_{xy}}{\sqrt{r_{yy}}}$$

As cited in Muchinsky (1996), the rationale for correcting the criterion and not the test variable goes back to Guilford (1954):

> In predicting criterion measures from test scores, one should not make a complete [double] correction for attenuation. Corrections should be made in the criterion only. On the one hand it is not a fallible criterion that we should aim to predict, including all its errors; it is a "true" criterion or the true component of the obtained criterion. On the other hand, we should not correct for errors in the test, because it is the fallible scores from which we must make predictions. We never know the true scores from which to predict. (p. 401)

Muchinsky (1996) provides comprehensive coverage on the topic of the different methods and rationale for correcting for attenuation.

So far, we have highlighted problems of attenuated and distorted correlation coefficients as a consequence of measurement error. Measurement error can manifest in other ways with unique and potentially serious consequences. For example, assume that measurements of a construct were taken every week during the course of a year. Assume further that the theoretical range of the construct is from 0 to 10, but the true score is 5 and remains perfectly stable across all measurement occasions. Thus, by graphing the trend line over time, it would remain perfectly parallel with the y-axis, as depicted in Figure 4.2.

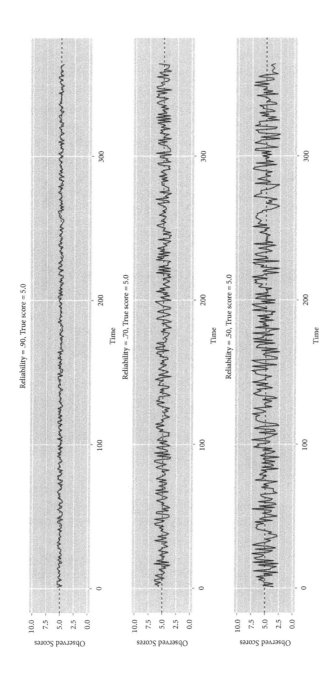

Figure 4.2 Reliability of measures depicted graphically over time.

The other trend lines in Figure 4.2 represent our observed measures with three different levels of random error (alpha = .50, .70, .90). The distance between the lines and the true score across measurement occasions represents measurement error. As expected, the variability around the true score increases with lower levels of reliability. When the reliability is .50, the observed values approach the anchor points, which can give false impressions that real trends exist. This is of particular relevance to social work research because it is usually feasible to have only a few measurement occasions in longitudinal research. Although CTT shows that these random errors will average out with an increased number of cases, we can be making serious mistakes when measurements for individuals are interpreted, such as a single-subject design, competency assessment, or clinical assessment.

Both Table 4.1 and Figure 4.2 show the consequences of measurement error are more severe when the reliability estimates are lower. The consequences of measurement error are smaller as reliability increases, but the consequences of error always exist until we achieve perfect reliability (1.0). Perfect reliability is something we strive to achieve, although we know it is not possible to achieve it. Although perfect reliability is unattainable, estimates of reliability in the .90s are attainable and definitely worth attaining. It is important that we be skeptical of mediocre threshold approaches.

Those of you who are familiar with SEM, factor analysis, or IRT know the value of different ways to account for measurement error. However, the use of such procedures does not eliminate error from our data. For example, although a scale may have been developed and analyzed carefully using any one of these procedures, it still produces data with measurement error. This is because measurement error manifests in our data and not in the actual measurement instrument. Now we can turn to a more detailed account of the sources and assessment of measurement error.

SOURCES OF ERROR

Both random and systematic measurement error can be traced to a variety of sources, but ultimately they all arise out of the activity of data collection (Viswanathan, 2005). In addition, our understanding of reliability and measurement error cannot be separated from theory. The theory underlying the constructs we measure is critical to the proper assessment of reliability. Specifically, we need to know or assume the nature of fluctuations in our measurements to distinguish true variance from measurement error. Certain constructs are expected to be highly stable over time, such as personality traits, whereas other constructs, such as emotional states, are less stable.

When we take measures of human behavior (broadly defined), we are assuming stability or consistency of the behavior within the study time frame. That is, we often hold that what we are measuring does not change over some conditions of observation (e.g., occasions) (Kane, 2011, p. 13). For example, when we examine the stability of measurements over time, we are assuming stability in the construct, and that the observed variation is attributable to random error. If we are studying personality traits using a self-rating system (e.g., cite a Big-Five measure), we would assume stability in any given set of traits because personality theory has established that traits are highly stable over time and occasions.

If weekly assessments of personality traits were obtained, it is unlikely we would obtain exactly the same score each time. The extent to which this variability is attributable to measurement error can be resolved only with theory. As Kane (2011) argues, "[there] is nothing in the data, as such, that forces us to treat the variability over occasions as error" (p. 13). In other words, the underlying theory of personality and personality assessment is required to determine what is true variance versus measurement error. If theory has established that personality traits are stable on a week-to-week basis, the variability is reasonably attributed to measurement error.

Other arguments are also possible. For example, the variability could represent real changes in the expression of personality traits or a combination of real changes and measurement error. However, based on the theory, it would be hard to justify any sort of real change in personality traits within this short period of time. On the other hand, if measurements were taken less frequently, such as every 2 or 3 years, the interpretation of variability—real change versus measurement error—becomes more challenging. This consideration of variability in our data indicates that reliability is not a property of the measure but a characteristic of our data. Thus, like validity, social work researchers are discouraged from characterizing a measure as being reliable or unreliable. The theory underlying our constructs should state or imply appropriate time intervals to minimize distortions in inferences regarding reliability. Constructs that show high levels of variability require more measurement occasions.

From applications of CTT, the measurement error we estimate and sometimes correct (adjust for statistically) is *random error*. The estimates of error in our data are summarized by reliability coefficients, which are essential for making judgments about the error in our data. It is helpful to identify the different types of random error, because that knowledge can guide us in selecting the most appropriate reliability coefficient.

The three major types of error include random response error, specific factor error, and transient error. We also discuss a special case of error called *idiosyncratic rater error*. This type of error can be the result of any of the three major types of error (i.e., random response, specific factor, and transient), but the source of the error is that of a rater in observational studies rather than a respondent to a scale, index, or exam.

It should be emphasized that the forgoing types of errors are considered random (vs. systematic) because they arise at random within a sample and tend to cancel out each other. However, it is not correct to assume that the actual mechanisms or processes that give rise to random error are themselves random. In fact, the mechanisms or processes that give rise to random error in general have an identifiable source of influence, including influences of the researcher or the procedure of measurement. In fact, the latter, referred to as *measurement reactivity,* is very common in social work research. In their classic text on psychometrics, Lord and Novick (1968) observed that we can perhaps repeat a measurement once or twice, but if we attempt further repetitions, the examinee's response changes substantially because of fatigue or practice effects (p. 13). Since then, numerous studies have found many different ways that measurement reactivity can manifest within a study. For example, Johnston (1999) found that a change in order of questions evoked higher anxiety scores among women with breast cancer (as cited in French and Sutton [2011]). Although emotions and psychological states can be affected easily by measurement reactivity, it is also important to consider that behavior is also influenced. For example, McCambridge and Day (2007) found that screening for alcohol use disorders leads to reductions in alcohol consumption for up to 2 to 3 months later (French & Sutton, 2011). This shows that measurement can be very powerful and can actually be a critical component of interventions. But, failure to pay careful attention to when emotions or behaviors may be influenced by our measurements can lead to very serious misinterpretations of findings.

The following discussion reviews and provides examples of the different classes of random error, including random response error, specific factor error, transient error, and idiosyncratic rater error.

Random Response Error

Random response error is considered *noise* attributable to the central nervous system of the respondent (Schmidt, Viswesvaran, & Ones, 2000). This noise reflects natural variations in attention and mental processing that occur during a measurement occasion. For example, continuing with personality assessment, we can assume that a person completing a lengthy self-rating will not give the same degree or mental processing to each item being rated. The difference in degree of attention or mental processing is considered random error, to the extent the variability is uncorrelated with any other variables. Some individuals may exhibit a fatigue effect in completing a lengthy questionnaire or rating. Thus, the degree of attention or mental processing would be compromised at later times during the measurement process, making it possible to correlate the variability with the serial position of items. Fatigue, however, would give rise to systematic error, not random response error. However, the error would be random response error if the degree of mental fluctuations observed at the beginning of the measurement occasion was consistent throughout the measurement occasions.

Specific Factor Error

Specific factor error relates to variance in responses to a specific type of item that is unrelated to the construct of interest (Hunter & Schmidt, 2004). Such errors arise through the interactions of respondents with items, scales, or raters (Schmidt et al., 2000, p. 908). Such errors arise typically from the interpretation of items based on wording. Thus, they are item specific and consistent across occasions for a given respondent (Barman, 2011).

Consider the Beck Depression Inventory—II (see Beck et al., 1996), which is one of the most widely used measures of depression. This questionnaire consists of 21 groups of statements. Respondents are instructed to read each group of statements and pick one statement from each group that best describes how they have been doing during the past 2 weeks. If several statements apply equally well, the respondent is instructed to circle the highest number for that group. The following contains one item from the inventory along with its respective group of statements, which provides a real-world context for considering specific factors error:

Punishment Feelings
0 I don't feel I am being punished
1 I feel I may be punished
2 I expect to be punished
3 I feel I am being punished

On review of these items, it should be quite clear that the statements with higher values represent higher levels of *punishment feelings*, which is considered one of the facets of depression. A careful conceptual analysis of these items can help reveal possible interpretations that might give rise to specific factors error. For example, consider a respondent who is concurrently involved with the legal system for some type of civil or criminal infraction. Such a respondent might, indeed, feel a sense of *punishment*. However, that sense of punishment is fundamentally different than the sense of punishment feelings that are considered to arise with depression. However, this inventory does not give any context or further instruction on how this item is intended to be interpreted. Differential interpretations of items would be considered specific factors error.

Specific factor error is of obvious concern with self-reporting, but it can also occur with observational measures. For example, specific factor error can occur easily when rating academic products (e.g., course participation or engagement). That is, the intention of the rater (course instructor) is to make an assessment of academic performance on specified dimensions of quality (e.g., kinds of questions raised, extent of active engagement, enthusiasm for the material). However, any given rating might be biased by the rater's overall appraisal of the individual as opposed to the target construct being measured. This particular bias in rating is considered a *halo effect* (Nunnally & Bernstein, 1994, p. 339). It is considered a specific factor error because what is being measured would not correlate with other items that measure the target construct (Schmidt, Le, & Ilies, 2003). When many items are used to measure the target construct, specific error tends to cancel out across the different items, but they replicate across measurement occasions (Schmidt et al., 2003).

Specific factor error is not commonly assessed in social work research, although the lack of attention to this kind of error should not imply that it is unimportant or nonexistent. In fact, in social work research, we often draw samples of persons with diverse backgrounds. Thus, the cultural lens that is brought to bear on the understanding and interpretations of items is an important source of specific factors error. One of the most practical starting points for identifying possible sources of specific factors error is by using *think-aloud* protocols during the measurement development phase. This involves using individuals who are representative of the target sample to talk out loud as they respond to a given questionnaire, providing interpretations in vivo to indicate their understanding of each item. Doing so can help identify possible sources of ambiguity that are the basis of specific factor error.

Transient Error

Another source of error not commonly considered in social work research is *transient error*. Transient error is the result of an interaction between respondents and measurement occasions. This type of error varies across measurement occasions but is consistent within a measurement occasion (Heggestad, George, & Reeve, 2006). According to Rozeboom (1966), "a substantial portion of the uncontrolled extraneous conditions that are presumably responsible for measurement error persist from one item to the next, thus inducing positive error correlation" (p. 415). Thus, the score variance can be attributed to other factors during that particular measurement occasion (e.g., mood states, emotional states, temporary health problems, crises or unusual conditions in the environment) that are not consistent at subsequent measurement occasions.

As an example of transient error, assume that an individual felt ill while taking an exam or completing a survey. That illness could influence the individual's ability to concentrate during this measurement occasion. Assume further that the individual's illness was resolved and the measurements were taken again a week or so later. The observed variance in the scores across the occasions would be the result of the illness, which is considered transient error (Heggestad et al., 2006). A consequence of transient error is that assessments of error based on cross-sectional data (e.g., coefficient alpha, split-half correlations) overestimate the reliability in a set of scores to the extent that they were influenced by transient error (Heggestad et al., 2006).

Although transient error is rarely discussed in the social work literature, it is likely quite common because we work with people who are often affected by the type of circumstances that can give rise to transient error. Unfortunately, a majority of the research in social work involves cross-sectional data, and transient error can only be assessed using test–retest methods. Transient error further establishes the fact that reliability is not a property of our measurement devices (e.g., scales), but instead is a property of our data.

Idiosyncratic Rater Error

Idiosyncratic rater error occurs in observational studies in which raters make observations based on a set of procedures and decision rules. For example, if we are conducting a systematic review or meta-analysis, rules need to be specified regarding which studies are included and excluded. A single person may carry out the entirety of the coding, but we need to make sure that the rules for inclusion and exclusion can be applied consistently by another coder. Other examples may involve examining classroom behaviors at fixed time intervals, rating the quality of specific clinical skills for a therapy, or assigning specific codes in qualitative research.

Idiosyncratic rater error occurs when raters make subjective assessments or deviate from the decision rules that are intended to ensure consistency among the raters. We want our raters to be fungible—that is, any given rater could be replaced by another rater to perform the measurement task in the same manner, observing and recording the same type of phenomena. The actual error could be attributed to the sources of error already discussed—for example, any rater may become fatigued and make a mistake in the measurement process (random response error). Or, the specific rules for taking measurements may be ambiguous, thus allowing for multiple interpretations (specific factors error).

Idiosyncratic rater error is complex because it essentially represents another unique source of error in our data. More specifically, assume we are administering an exam or assessing clinical skills. We need to be concerned about the consistency of administration. We also need to be concerned about the consistency of those who are either grading the exam or rating the clinical skills. Thus, a comprehensive reliability analysis would involve a reliability analysis of both the respondents and the raters.

ASSESSING AND QUANTIFYING ERROR

All measurements produce data with some degree of error. The amount of error tends to be greater when measuring human characteristics than when measuring physical objects, and the kinds of error associated with data representing human characteristics tend to be more complex than data of physical objects. The amount of error is summarized using various correlational methods to produce *reliability coefficients*. Because we have different types of error, no single coefficient can provide a summary of the overall error.

Although it is important to understand the amount of error contained in one's data, resources and time constraints force researchers to make decisions about which kinds of error can be assessed. Although there is no *correct* decision in this dilemma, such decisions are best informed by strong theoretical knowledge of the concepts being studied, and the underlying theory and principles of reliability and validity. We limit our presentation of reliability coefficients to those that are understood within the framework of CTT, because social work relies almost exclusively on CTT to understand random response error, specific factors error, and transient error.

Within CTT, we have three major classes of reliability coefficients: equivalence, stability, and equivalence and stability. The correlational methods for addressing random response error and specific factors error are the same, but different procedures are necessary for assessing transient error. Because the assessment of random response and specific factors error are the same, the resulting reliability coefficient does not differentiate the amount of error attributable to the unique sources. Such differentiation of error requires a different framework of reliability analysis: generalizability theory (see Hambleton, Swaminathan, & Rogers, 1991). Generalizability holds an important place in social science research. However, it is rarely used in social work research and is beyond the scope of this handbook. Suggested readings are provided at the end of this chapter to guide those of you who are interested in acquiring knowledge of G-theory.

The following discussion focuses on the major types of reliability coefficients for quantifying the three major sources of error: coefficient of equivalence (CE), coefficient of stability (CS), and the coefficient of equivalence and stability (CES). We then cover interrater reliability, which is used to account for the special case of idiosyncratic rater error. Next, we talk about how to use reliability coefficients in calculating a standard error of measurement. The standard error of measurement is used to understand and interpret the error of an individual score. It should be noted that the standard error of measurement is commonly abbreviated as SEM. To avoid confusion with structural equation modeling, which shares the same abbreviation, we will use the full spelling of the standard error of measurement.

Coefficient of Equivalence (CE)

The CE is used to compute the reliability of different versions of the same test. The same version may be two separately constructed versions of the same test (i.e., parallel forms), or different versions may be constructed by dividing the same test systematically (i.e., split-half). The CE assesses specific factor and random response error but not transient error (Schmidt et al., 2003). The estimation procedure for equivalence is Pearson's r.

Parallel Forms

In some circumstances it may be possible to use the same format to develop two different measures that measure the same construct. For example, state motor vehicle departments have five or six versions of a test measuring knowledge of driving regulations. Each test is comparable, meaning that one's driving ability would be measured at the same level regardless of which test is taken. When persons seek a social work license and take the national examination through the Association of Social Work Boards, they are assigned one of three different versions of the same test. Because the tests were developed in the same way and are presumably measuring the same thing, we expect the scores on one version of the measure to correlate highly to the other versions of the same measure. The extent to which they correlate represents an estimate of *parallel forms* reliability.

Split-Half Reliability

Split-half reliability involves dividing a measure in half randomly or systematically and assessing the extent to which each half is equivalent. For example, if we have a 30-item scale, we could select every other item or randomly select 15 items to constitute one set of measurements, with the remaining 15 items constituting the second set of measurements. The correlation between these sets of measurements yields split-half reliability. Because reliability is influenced by the number of items contained in the measure, split-half reliability is not appropriate for scales or other measurement procedures that contain only a small set of items, and often a correction for attenuation is applied (Nunnally & Bernstein, 1994). Split-half reliability estimates are, therefore, rarely used.

Coefficient of Stability

The CS refers to consistency of estimates over measurement occasions, such as from time 1 to time 2. This estimate is based on the assumption that no change should have occurred between the measurement occasions. Thus, if the CS is high, this suggests no reactivity to measurement and a high degree of reliability (Madsen, 2004). The CS assesses transient and random response error but not specific factor error (Schmidt et al., 2003). Like the estimation procedure, the CS is estimated using Pearson's *r*.

Test–retest analysis is the primary procedure for making this assessment. It involves taking measurements on one occasion (time 1), repeating the measurement process at a later time (time 2), and then assessing the consistency of the responses across time using correlational procedures. This procedure assumes that the meaning of the construct remains the same over the time period assessed.

Like the other forms of reliability (and validity), this type of analysis requires a strong understanding of the target construct, which is ultimately informed by the theory in which the construct is embedded. More specifically, because we are typically assessing dynamic constructs (i.e., constructs that exhibit some degree of change over time), it is critical to specify the time frame in which changes in measurements from time 1 to time 2 are expected to be imperceptible or negligible.

No general guidelines exist for specifying a time frame, because different time frames exist for different constructs. Perhaps the best advice for selecting the time frame is to have the longest duration of time between measurement occasions that would be practical and consistent with theory. For example, personality traits are considered to be highly stable across time and occasions, which suggests that we could safely specify a time frame in weeks or months. On the other hand, we cannot repeat the measurements within too short a period of time (e.g., 5 days), because respondents are likely to remember what they originally answered, and this introduces serious threats to validity. That is, the measurements may be interpreted as an indicator of memory as opposed to personality.

If the measure is particularly lengthy, the respondent may come to feel a sense of boredom, increasing the number of random response errors. Thus, one might select a time frame of approximately 2 weeks. This time frame is appropriate for personality traits but not necessarily other constructs. For example, if we are measuring withdrawal symptoms among persons who are dependent on alcohol, we could reasonably expect notable changes over the course of hours. Thus, if we are concerned with the stability of measurements in this research, we might consider the time frame to be less than a single hour.

Coefficient of Equivalence and Stability

Although the CE and the CS are used for assessing different subsets of our three major types of error—random response, specific factors, and transient—the CES is the only coefficient that estimates the magnitude of all three types of error, which makes it an ideal (albeit underused) coefficient (Schmidt et al., 2003). Estimating the CES involves correlating two parallel forms of a measure on two different occasions and computing the CES based on the following equation:

$$CES = \rho(1A,\ 2B) = \rho(2A,\ 1B)$$

Measurement reactivity refers to how psychological measurement can affect thoughts, feelings, and behavior (French & Sutton, 2011). If we assume that measurement reactivity is not a problem (e.g., fatigue or anxiety resulting from the measurement process), the assumptions can be relaxed and the same scale can be administered on two different occasions. The relaxing of assumptions has appeal because it is often the case that parallel forms are not available, giving rise to an alternate method for computing the CES. This involves administering a measure on two different occasions and then splitting the scale to form parallel half scales. Schmidt et al. (2003) provide detailed descriptions for computing the CES for parallel half scales and scales with an odd number of items.in this equation, A and B denote parallel forms of a single measure, and 1 and 2 represent the time points (time 1 and time 2, respectively). A full breakdown of this equation is provided by Schmidt et al. (2003, pp. 211–213). This equation assumes that a scale can be split into parallel half scales, and the properties of the half scale (i.e., standard deviations and the CE) remain unchanged across occasion.

Internal Consistency

Estimates of internal consistency refer to the interrelatedness among the items of a measure (Cortina, 1993). They help us understand the extent to which the multiple items making up a measure produce similar scores. The most popular way of estimating internal consistency in social work research is by using Cronbach's alpha (Cronbach, 1951). Cronbach's alpha is the average of all split-half reliabilities—that is, the correlation between two halves of a scale, which is then adjusted to reflect the reliability of the full scale. It is conceptually equivalent to the correlation between two parallel forms administered on the same occasion; therefore, it is classified as a CE estimate.

Estimates of internal consistency do not provide evidence for the unidimensionality of a measure. As noted earlier in the domain-sampling model and explained in detail by Cortina (1993), any given set of items can be highly interrelated and multidimensional. The overall number of items also influences estimates of internal consistency. In general, scales that have more items have higher levels of internal consistency.

In social work research, an internal consistency estimate of .70 is widely regarded as an acceptable level of internal consistency. It is also commonly believed that values closer to 1.0 are highly desirable. We recommend that social work researchers not rely on these *rules of thumb* and instead consider the implications of each internal consistency estimate carefully in relation to the construct being measured, the characteristics of the measurement device, and the characteristics of the sample.

To illustrate the problem with using these rules of thumb, consider two different measures of the same construct that are administered to the same sample. Estimates of internal consistency for both measures are .70. A comparison of these two values alone would give the impression that the internal consistency estimates are exactly the same. However, if one measure contains five items and the other measure contains 50 items, they are clearly not comparable because, as noted earlier, estimates of internal consistency are affected (positively) by the number of items and by the magnitudes of the correlations, which is how two such different measures could have the same measure of reliability.

Another problem of internal consistency that is often misunderstood is that values closer to 1.0 are not necessarily desirable, despite numerous claims in the published research that suggest otherwise. In fact, values that approach 1.0 can be indicative of serious problems with the measure. More specifically, assume we have a measure with an internal consistency estimate of 1.0. Although the rule of thumb suggests that a higher value is better, in this case all the items are perfectly correlated with each other. In other words, each item is completely redundant with the other items, so they are reflections of exactly the same facet of the target construct. This problem is likely a result of the phrasing of the items, which gives the impression they are conceptually distinct but are actually redundant. Thus, estimates that approach the value 1.0 may contain important redundancies that inflate artificially the intended meaning of this type of reliability estimate.

High estimates of internal consistency deserve the same level of scrutiny as low estimates. It is important to examine the conceptual distinctiveness of each item. Researchers who develop or administer a given scale may have expert knowledge of the target construct and may see conceptual differences among the various items. However, it is important that the conceptual analysis be considered from the viewpoint of the respondent, who may not see such nuances. This idea establishes further the important point that reliability is not a property of a measure, but a characteristic of the sample data, which can be influenced by many factors.

Interrater Reliability

When people complete a scale, index, examination, or some other form of measurement, they include some amount of measurement error that can be classified as random response, specific factor, or transient error. As discussed previously, sometimes we have raters who make evaluative assessments or judgments, which requires us to understand the consistency of the evaluations or judgments. This is done through test–retest reliability analyses. We next provide an overview of the major strategies and coefficients, and the recommended readings provide resources to inform test–retest analyses not covered in this handbook.

We use the term *objects* broadly to refer to anything being rated (e.g., behaviors, characteristics of people, activities, studies); the term *raters* refers to persons who are performing standardized assessments or coding activities. When conducting an interrater reliability analysis, we seek to quantify the degree of agreement between two or more raters who make independent ratings about the characteristics of a set of objects. In other words, we want to quantify the degree to which the raters are providing similar ratings.

An interrater reliability analysis may be a focus of the research. For example, this type of research is common in research on new diagnostic criteria for mental disorders (e.g., hyperactivity or distractibility—attention deficit hyperactivity disorder). Other times, interrater reliability analysis may not be the focus, but an essential part of the research. For example, a meta-analysis involves the selection of published and unpublished studies according to a set of inclusionary and exclusionary criteria. It is necessary to determine the extent to which the inclusionary and exclusionary criteria are applied consistently. The focus of the research is not on interrater reliability, but is an essential part of the study.

Regardless of whether interrater reliability analysis is the focus of the research or a central component of a broader study, it is essential that design issues associated with interrater reliability be considered carefully before data are collected because the design ultimately influences the computation and interpretation of the results. According to Hallgren (2012), four basic designs exist, which are depicted in Table 4.2.

Table 4.2 shows different permutations of rating designs based on whether all objects are rated by multiple raters or whether a subset of objects is rated by multiple raters. A number of important decisions can be inferred from this table. Looking first at the columns of Table 4.2, we

Table 4.2 Designs for Assigning Coders to Subjects for Interrater Reliability Studies

		All subjects rated by multiple coders				Subset of subjects rated by multiple coders		
		Coder A	Coder B	Coder C		Coder A	Coder B	Coder C
Design fully crossed	Subject 1	X	X	X	Subject 1	X	X	X
	Subject 2	X	X	X	Subject 2	X	X	
	Subject 3	X	X	X	Subject 3	X	X	X
	Subject 4	X	X	X	Subject 4			
		Coder A	Coder B	Coder C		Coder A	Coder B	Coder C
Design not fully crossed	Subject 1		X	X	Subject 1	X	X	
	Subject 2	X		X	Subject 2	X		
	Subject 3		X	X	Subject 3		X	X
	Subject 4	X	X		Subject 4		X	

Note: X indicates the ratings were provided by a given coder to the corresponding subject. Reproduced from Hallgren, K. A. (2012).

must determine whether all the objects will be rated by multiple raters or whether a subset of objects will be rated by multiple raters. Although having all ratings of all objects by all raters provides more complete data for examining reliability, it can be costly and impractical, especially in large study designs when multiple attributes of objects are being rated. The subset strategy may be used to generalize to the full sample. In reference to the rows of Table 4.2, we can also consider whether the objects will be rated by the same set of raters (design fully crossed) or whether different objects are rated by different subsets of coders (design not fully crossed). Although fully crossed designs allow for the identification of biases between raters and are easier to analyze, this type of design requires more resources to implement.

The major strategies for analysis of interrater reliability data are Cohen's kappa (κ) and the intraclass correlation (ICC). The selection of these reliability coefficients will be based on the rating design and the type of measurement data (i.e., nominal, ordinal, continuous, ratio). Cohen's kappa and the many derivations of this statistic measure the level of agreement between raters for categorical ratings, with a correction for chance. The original Cohen's kappa is suitable only for fully crossed designs with exactly two raters (see Hallgren, 2012), which has given rise to many other derivations of this statistic. This has evoked a large body of literature, given the various study characteristics involved in interrater reliability analyses. The ICC is the primary strategy for assessing interrater reliability when the level of measurement is at the ordinal, continuous, and ratio levels (Hallgren, 2012). A number of variants exist to account for multiple raters and different rating designs.

STANDARD ERROR OF MEASUREMENT

So far, issues of reliability and measurement error have been discussed relative to the needs of social work researchers. This discussion has focused on the reliability of a set of scores—that is, sample data. However, when measurements are used in practice, we often make interpretations of individual scores on standardized tests, such as intelligence tests, personality inventories, and license examinations. When decisions are made based on individual test scores, issues of reliability need to be considered.

The statistics reviewed thus far reflect reliability of the sample data, not a score for any given individual. For example, assume that an individual is completing a standardized licensing exam. The stability of the exam (i.e., test–retest) was found to be .80, indicating unreliability across measurement occasions. This value indicates the measurement error in the data, but the reliability coefficient is a summary of the internal consistency for a set of scores, not a measure of the error in a given individual's score. It would be helpful to know approximately how far away the observed score is for that individual's true score, which would require that individual to repeat the test on multiple occasions, with the average score being the best approximation of her or his true score. This is not practical, because it would be resource intensive and would likely give rise to numerous forms of test reactivity.

A statistic that aids our understanding of the reliability of a given score is the standard error of measurement. The standard error of measurement is used to convey a range of scores that is a plausible estimate of the individual's true score. This range of scores is presented as a confidence interval around the individual's observed score, which is based on the individual's observed score and the reliability of the test. The standard error of measurement is estimated by multiplying the sample standard deviation times the square root of one less the reliability coefficient.

$$SEM = \sigma \sqrt{1 - r}$$

The confidence interval provides a quantitative estimate of the amount of precision of our score. A 68% confidence band is approximately equal to one standard deviation on either side of the mean. This level of confidence is typically adequate for scientific studies. A 95% confidence band is approximately equal to two standard deviations. This level of confidence is used in clinical work.

As a worked example, assume we are measuring a construct with a 20-item scale made up of 5-point Likert–type responses (range, 0–4 points). An overall score is obtained by summing the scores (range, 0–80 points). Let's say this scale was administered to a large sample of clients, but for clinical purposes we are interested only in the interpretation for a single respondent. For simplicity, we assume the standard deviation of scores for this scale was 5.0, with an internal consistency estimate of .85. Note that any kind of reliability coefficient may be used.

However, the type of coefficient used in calculating the SEM can make a difference because each type of coefficient is measuring the effect of different sources of error. This should be considered in both the selection of a coefficient and the interpretation of the standard error of measurement.

Assume that a given client had an observed score of 15 points. Using the previous equation, we can compute the SEM:

$$\text{SEM} = \sigma\sqrt{1-r} = 5\sqrt{1-.85} = 1.94$$

We can now use this value to construct a confidence band around the respondent's score. We assume that a 68% confidence band is approximately equal to one standard deviation on either side of the mean, and a 95% confidence band is approximately equal to two standard deviations on either side of the mean.

- 68% Confidence band: 15 ± (standard error of measurement) = 15 ± 1.94 = 13.06 to 16.94. *Interpretation:* Chances are 68 out of 100 that an observed score of 15 points falls in the range between 13.06 points and 16.94 points.
- 95% Confidence band: 15 ± 2 (standard error of measurement) = 15 ± 3.88 = 11.12 to 18.88. *Interpretation:* Chances are 95 out of 100 that an observed score of 15 points falls in the range between 11.12 points and 18.88 points.

Although researchers may not use the standard error of measurement on a regular basis, it is important that it be reported in measurement studies, particularly for those measures that are encouraged for use in practice settings. Doing so helps practitioners have a range of plausible scores based on the observed score, which can be particularly helpful whenever a test or measurement is used for decision-making purposes, especially when a cutoff score is used for making critical decisions.

It should be noted that the standard error of measurement is based on a reliability coefficient, making it important that researchers select carefully the most appropriate reliability statistic for computing and reporting the standard error of measurement. The most appropriate reliability statistic is one that reflects the most likely kind of error implied by the theory and circumstances of the study. If the researcher suspects different kinds of error, it is wise to use a CES measure of reliability. However, because calculating CES reliability is sometimes not feasible, an alternative is to calculate two different SEMs using different reliability coefficients, such as a CE and a CS measure of reliability.

Alternatives to Classical Test Theory

This chapter has used CTT as the framework for understanding reliability and measurement error. As discussed previously, social work researchers rely almost exclusively on CTT. This is certainly no criticism; CTT is aptly suited for nearly all measurement-related issues in social work research. However, as we conclude this chapter, we feel compelled to highlight two other frameworks for understanding reliability and measurement error—G-theory and IRT—because they each shed additional light on the difficult and disturbing role of error in social work research and theory in general.

Generalizability Theory

Generalizability theory, or G-theory, is considered a liberalization of CTT because it provides a framework for quantifying and distinguishing "sources of inconsistencies in observed scores that arise, or could arise, over replications of a measurement procedure" (Brennan, 2011, p. 2). With CTT, the error-free measurement is conceptualized as a *true score,* whereas with G-theory it is understood as the *universe score.* The underlying premise of G-theory involves the extent to which one can generalize from a sample of observations to a universe of randomly sampled observations. Thus, reliability of observations depends ultimately on the universe (or even universes) about which inferences are to be made. The universes involve a clear specification of the conditions associated with different observations, which is considered the *universe of admissible observations.* Different universes have different conditions and, therefore, may exhibit variability in the extent to which generalizations can be made. Observations are considered *dependable* if they allow accurate inferences to be made about the universe of admissible observations.

Although CTT remains the central framework for virtually all aspects of measurement in social work research, it is necessary to recognize that a serious limitation of the CTT equation ($X = T + E$) is that the error component (E) includes many different types of error, but only one type of error is estimated at a time. A primary advantage of G-theory is the ability to estimate the proportion of variance in observed scores that are attributable to many other factors (e.g., test setting, test forms, test items, time). G-theory relies heavily on analysis of variance approaches and variance component estimation to isolate different factors that influence measurements. To date, very few studies involving G-theory have been published in social work journals. Gehlert (1994) provides an excellent overview of the applicability of G-theory to social work research and practice.

Item Response Theory

IRT views responses to items—and, consequently, the interpretation of error—in a way that is fundamentally different than CTT. In CTT, any given item of a scale can, in theory, be replaced by another item that is derived from the same *universe* of items. Each item is assumed to have the same strength of relationship with the latent variable it represents (latent variables are covered in greater detail in Chapter 5). Within the CTT framework, each item of a scale or measure is assumed to be equal.

Although the focus of analysis in CTT is on the test or scale, the focus of IRT is on the individual items, which contribute different levels or amount of information, depending on the difficulty of the item (one-parameter IRT models), item discrimination (two-parameter IRT models), or the ability of one to guess the correct response to an item (three-parameter IRT models). IRT is used to gather this information for each item of a test or scale independent of the individuals who are responding to them. For example, an IRT analysis is very appropriate for use in a standardized licensure examination, such as the one administered by the Association of Social Work Boards. This analysis would reveal the difficulty of items (relative to other items), the extent to which any given item discriminates who has the knowledge being assessed, and the ease or probability of guessing.

The concept of reliability in IRT relates to *precision* of a given item. Precision is considered a continuous function of the measured construct and is usually depicted by item information curves (referred to as *ICCs*, but should not be confused with the same acronym for intraclass correlation) or functions, indicating the range for which an item *discriminates* among individuals (Edelen & Reeve, 2007). The reliability coefficients from CTT provide an estimate for a set of scores, whereas IRT focuses on the individual items.

A primary advantage of IRT over CTT is the information derived for individual items, allowing researchers to optimize the instrument for a particular purpose. For example, it is possible to use the information from IRT-based analysis to construct shorter tests by selecting the items that contain the greatest levels of discrimination. IRT can also be used for adaptive testing, which is a computer-based assessment that adjusts the difficulty of exam questions during an examination to establish a score that is closest to the individual's true score. This type of adaptive testing is simply not feasible within a CTT framework. IRT is especially suitable for educational environments for the development of examinations, particularly when threshold or cutoff scores are established for decision-making purposes.

GENERAL SUGGESTIONS FOR IMPROVING SCORE RELIABILITY

In the following list are general strategies to help reduce error and thus improve reliability in our data with the measures we use. These are general strategies that are more applicable in some measurement contexts than others.

- Ensure the measure has a clear and standardized set of instructions for administration. Members of the research team who are administering the test or conducting the ratings must be trained.
- Make sure each measurement item and instructions are written clearly in the language of the subjects or respondents. When using a questionnaire, it is a good idea to provide an example that shows exactly how to respond to the items. Different interpretations of an item introduce a source of error that erodes the reliability of the data.
- Pilot test the measure and solicit feedback from subjects or respondents comparable with those to be studied. It is essential to understand how subjects or respondents are interpreting the items. A think-aloud style of investigation can be used, which involves having subjects or respondents speak their thoughts out loud when responding to measurement items.

- Increase the number of items for a measure, which increases measures of reliability. Measures with 10 items are generally precise with high reliability, and carefully constructed measures with half that many items often work well.
- Identify ways to reduce administrative errors when recording data. For example, sometimes ratings are made on paper and are then entered manually into a computer. Consider ways to use technology to avoid multiple entry processes.
- Use multiple measures of the same construct for purposes of triangulation. This strategy is a good way to help identify possible sources of systematic error.
- Be skeptical of relying on general rules of thumb or cutoffs for reliability scores. Interpretations and decisions based on reliability should be considered in context of the substantive theory being studied and the underlying measurement theory of the concept.

KEY POINTS

- Reliability refers to the consistency of measurements when the testing procedure or scale is repeated for a sample of individuals or groups.
- Reliability is a necessary but not sufficient condition for validity. It is more amenable to assessment than validity, but validity is the paramount concern in measurement.
- The domain-sampling model establishes the foundation for drawing reliable measures. The model assumes an infinite pool of items but works well with large samples of items.
- Random error is a class of errors that is not correlated with the construct, other measures, or anything else under study. Random errors distribute symmetrically around the true value. The three major types of random error include random response error, specific factor error, and transient error.
- Systematic error exists when measures concentrate around alternative values instead of the true value. In other words, the observed scores are not distributed symmetrically around

the true score; instead, they are biased consistently upward or downward.

- The consequences of measurement error are less as reliability increases, but the consequences of error always exist.
- The coefficient of stability refers to the consistency of measurements over time, which is based on a test–retest design. Pearson's *r* is used for assessing stability.
- The CE refers to the reliability of different versions of the same test. Pearson's *r* is used for assessing equivalence.
- The CES is the only coefficient that estimates the magnitude of all three types of random error, which makes it an ideal (albeit underused) coefficient (Schmidt et al., 2003). Estimating the CES involves correlating two parallel forms of a measure on two different occasions.
- Systematic error cannot be estimated or corrected after the data have been collected.
- A statistic that aids our understanding of the reliability of a given score is the SEM.
- CTT dominates the social work research and is aptly suited for nearly all measurement-related issues in social work research. G-theory and IRT offer other perspectives to understanding measurement error.

RECOMMENDED AND CLASSIC READINGS

American Educational Research Association, American Psychological Association, and National Council on Measurement in Education. (2014). *Standards for educational and psychological testing.* Washington, DC: American Educational Research Association.

Bollen, K., & Lennox, R. (1991). Conventional wisdom on measurement: A structural equation perspective. *Psychological Bulletin, 110*(2), 305–314.

Brennan, R. (2000). (Mis)conceptions about generalizability theory. *Educational Measurement: Issues and Practice, 19*(1), 5–10.

Brennan, R. L. (2011). Generalizability theory and classical test theory. *Applied Measurement in Education, 24*, 1–21.

Cortina, J. M. (1993). What is coefficient alpha? An examination of theory and applications. *Journal of Applied Psychology, 78*(1), 98–104.

Cronbach, L. J. (1950). Further evidence on response sets and test design. *Emotional and Psychological Measurement, 10*, 3–31.

Cronbach, L. J. (1951). Coefficient alpha and the internal structure of tests. *Psychometrika, 16*(3), 297–334.

Frisbie, D. A. (2005). Measurement 101: Some fundamentals revisited. *Educational Measurement: Issues and Practice, 24*(1), 21–28. [Note: This article provides excellent foundation information for measurement issues in general, with exceptionally useful information on reliability.]

Green, S. B., Lissitz, R. W., & Mulaik, S. A. (1977). Limitations of coefficient alpha as an index of test unidimensionality. *Educational and Psychological Measurement, 37*(4), 827–838.

Kane, M. (2011). The errors of our ways. *Journal of Educational Measurement, 48*(1), 12–30.

Miller, M. B. (1995). Coefficient alpha: A basic introduction from the perspective of classical test theory and structural equation modeling. *Structural Equation Modeling, 2*(3), 255–273.

Schmidt, F. L., & Hunter, J. E. (1996). Measurement error in psychological research: Lessons from 26 research scenarios. *Psychological Methods, 1*(2), 199–223. [Note: Schmidt has made many important contributions to the measurement literature—in particular with regard to issues of reliability. He is a strong proponent of making corrections for measurement error, and many of his articles provide both a compelling case and practical strategies.]

Schmidt, F. L., & Hunter, J. E. (1999). Theory testing and measurement error. *Intelligence, 27*(3), 183–198.

Schmidt, F. L., Le, H., & Ilies, R. (2003). Beyond alpha: An empirical examination of the effects of different sources of measurement error on reliability estimates for measures of individual differences constructs. *Psychological Methods, 8*(2), 206–224.

Schmidt, F. L., Viswesvaran, C., & Ones, D. (2000). Reliability is not validity and validity is not reliability. *Personnel Psychology, 53*(4), 901–912.

5

Latent Variables

Those who think "Science is Measurement" should search Darwin's
works for numbers and equations.

—David Hunter Hubel

Many concepts that social work researchers study cannot be observed
or measured directly. Concepts such as self-esteem, depression, and job
satisfaction are just a few of numerous examples. These concepts are
called *latent variables*. They are *latent* in the sense they are hidden from
direct observation or they are hypothetical constructs hypothesized to
facilitate scientific explanation.

The analysis of latent variables has become easier during the past
two decades with the advancement of point-and-click computer applications. Although computer applications have eased the technical bur-
dens involved in the analysis of latent variables, these programs are
unable to—and will never be able to—address the substantive conceptual issues critical in the measurement of latent variables. This inherent shortcoming is apparent from the number of serious errors revealed
through the review by Guo et al. (2008) of studies published by social
work researchers.

In this chapter we provide a conceptual overview of latent variables.
Following the recommendation of Borsboom (2008), we maintain a

distinction between latent-variable models and latent-variable theories. This distinction is important because researchers too often apply statistical models of latent variables that are inconsistent or incompatible with the conceptual linkages between the data and real world as expressed or assumed by the theories. Our focus throughout this chapter is primarily on the conceptual and theoretical issues central to latent-variable measurement. There are excellent texts available that focus more on the technical aspects of latent-variable modeling (Bollen, 1989; Kline, 2010; Schumacker & Lomax, 2004).

The chapter is organized into five main sections. First, we clarify the distinction between latent and manifest variables. Second, we describe key principles of latent-variable theory, with an emphasis on dimensionality and causality. Third, we briefly introduce the strategies available for analyzing latent variables. Fourth, we discuss the evidence for validity with latent variables. Fifth, we discuss issues of reliability stemming from the use of single-item measures and item parcels. We conclude by underscoring the key points that have the potential to affect theory.

LATENT AND MANIFEST VARIABLES

Latent variables are unobserved variables inferred from hypothesized data patterns of manifest variables. Manifest variables are measured through one or more of the five human senses: sight, smell, taste, touch, and hearing. We hypothesize the existence of latent variables because they help to reduce the complexity of data, simplify the testing of theory, and increase the accuracy of empirical results. Large numbers of manifest variables can be theorized and modeled to represent a single, underlying latent variable or a small number of underlying latent variables and the relationships among all these variables.

For example, a theorist might hypothesize that workers' "commitment" to an organization causes them to be more "satisfied" with their employment. Mowday, Steers, and Porter (1979) measured the latent variable commitment with 15 manifest variables. Brayfield and Rothe (1951) measured the latent variable satisfaction with 17 manifest variables. By modeling these manifest variables as functions of their respective latent variables and regressing satisfaction on commitment, researchers simplify the data immensely and test the theory more directly.

Perhaps the most basic distinction between manifest and latent variables is that all manifest variables include measurement error whereas latent variables are typically measured without random measurement error. This is made possible because the random measurement error associated with the manifest variables is identified and removed from the relationships between the latent variable and its manifest variables, which results in what is called an *error-free estimate* of the latent variable.

The ability of social work researchers to measure error-free latent variables and test theories concomitantly by interrelating those latent variables is an important advancement over traditional methods of first evaluating measures and then developing models independently with those measures to test theories. The random error identified during the evaluation of measures is almost always ignored when testing theory and drawing conclusions from those results. Traditional statistical models assume the measures are totally error free, and researchers rarely made adjustments for the previously assessed error.

As we move forward in our discussion of latent variables, it is important to be clear about what *error-free* measurement is and is not. Error-free measurement is essentially a correction for attenuation based on CTT, which means the random and specific error from each manifest measurement has been estimated and removed. Although adjustments for random and specific error are inherent in latent-variable models, they are not incorporated within traditional correlation and regression models of manifest variables. It has been recommended that corrections for attenuation be applied routinely to manifest variables (see Schmidt, 2010), but this is practiced rarely in social work research. Thus, error-free measurement does not mean that systematic or conceptual errors have been removed. It means that random error has been removed. Although statistical adjustments to remove random and specific errors are helpful, it is much more preferable to make direct adjustments to our measures or measurement processes to minimize all forms of error. In other words, it is better to focus on changing the measure that may be a potential source of error (e.g., improving the clarity of instructions and reducing ambiguity among the items), and is far more beneficial than applying statistical corrections.

Theories are enhanced with latent variables because of their more abstract nature. Some researchers limit their study myopically to a manifest variable even though the variable has been conceptualized in theory as a latent variable. Howell (2008) offers an example in the study of sex differences relative to extraversion. Biological sex is almost always regarded as a manifest variable. However, extraversion is clearly a latent variable, and theories of sex differences in extraversion are not concerned with the presence or absence of a Y chromosome. Rather, sex is used as a proxy variable of "socialization, role-modeling, cultural expectations, sex-bias, and the like. Because a child is male or female, different outcomes accrue, and it is these outcomes that underlie the logic of studying sex differences in this context" (Howell, 2008, p. 98).

In this example, we are looking at the probabilistic outcomes of sex according to the theory of extraversion. There are two problems when using biological sex as a proxy. First, the measure of biological sex is dichotomous whereas extraversion is continuous. The loss of variance in using a dichotomous variable in place of a continuous variable is a source of error. Second, the worth of these outcomes depends on how closely related the modal responses of males and females are to the average levels of male and female extraversion. Discrepancies between these modes and averages introduce more error.

The logic justifying the use of sex as a proxy for extraversion can also be applied to age as a proxy for developmental periods, to race as a proxy for poverty, and many other examples in which stereotypes or modal differences across categories of people are accepted as representing real differences in theoretical constructs. It is important to recognize the limitations of using manifest variables as indicators of latent variables. This is a matter that should be dictated by substantive theory and not by stereotypes or the misplaced allure of direct observation and convenience of measurement.

KEY PRINCIPLES OF LATENT-VARIABLE THEORY

It is essential that latent variables be grounded in theory. The importance of theory to latent variables was spelled out initially by Cronbach and Meehl (1955) and Loevinger (1957), and was reinforced eloquently by Messick (1989). The meaning and relevance of constructs and relationships comes from the theories in which they are couched. Unfortunately, the requisite role of theory is too often given short shrift or ignored. We describe why it is vital to ground latent-variable constructs and their measures explicitly in theory.

First, it is important for facilitating unambiguous interpretations that latent variables have the property of unidimensionality. Dimensionality refers to the number of latent variables needed to account for the correlations among the manifest measures, so unidimensionality means that the correlations among a set of measures result from a single latent variable. Although it is essential to produce empirical evidence in support of a unidimensional hypothesis, ultimately, as we make clear later, the dimensionality of latent variables is established through theory.

Second, it is critical that the causal hypotheses defining latent-variable models be consistent with the assumptions underlying the guiding theoretical framework (Borsboom, 2008). The latent-variable constructs studied in social work and social science in general are consistent with one of two fundamentally different types of latent-variable models. The most widely used model is referred to as a *reflective model* in the sense that the manifest measures result from or reflect the latent variable. The much less frequently used model is referred to as *formative model* in the sense that the manifest measures cause or form the latent variable. As will be made clear in the following discussion, invalid results and confusion arise from applying a reflective model to a formative construct or from applying a formative model to a reflective construct.

Dimensionality

To order people based on a specified attribute, observe individual differences, create groups, and establish meaningful associations between variables, it is necessary the variables be unidimensional (Hattie, 1985). A unidimensional measure is composed of items that measure the same ability, achievement, attitude, or some other type of latent variable (Hattie, 1985). This means that the items used in unidimensional measures have homogeneity. Items that are homogenous "have but a single common factor among them that are related to the underlying factor . . . in a linear manner" (Green et al., 1977, p. 830). This is not to suggest that it is meaningless to study multidimensional constructs, but each dimension of a multidimensional construct could be and, in general, should be measured as a distinct factor. Theory dictates the relationships among those factors.

Unidimensionality is a basic assumption in measurement. Many of the constructs measured in social work research are conceptually complex, meaning that a given construct may contain distinct subconstructs (McGrath, 2005). (Please note that *subconstructs* can be used interchangeably with *dimensions*.) Depression, for example, is sometimes formulated as a unidimensional construct and other times as a complex construct. As a unidimensional construct, all the variability in the manifest measures is determined by the unitary construct of depression. As a multidimensional construct composed of affective depression and behavioral depression, the variability in observed data is explained by these two distinct but related dimensions of depression.

Using the example of depression, we are not interested in debating whether depression ought to be specified as a single, unified construct or a conceptually complex construct composed of two or more subconstructs (used synonymously with *subordinate factor* and *dimensions*). This is a matter of substantive theory, which precedes all measurement debates. Rather, the point to be made is that any single numeric value derived from a measure should represent a unidimensional construct. Thus, conceptually complex constructs require measures that tap each separate dimension uniquely. Theory can then guide us with regard to whether it is potentially worthwhile to model a higher order factor or to work exclusively with the distinct dimensions.

A higher order factor is when a set of subordinate factors fit together in a hierarchical fashion (Figure 5.1). As displayed in Figure 5.1, we have three subordinate factors measured with a specific set of manifest variables. These subordinate factors are all intercorrelated and can be modeled as separate variables. These subordinate factors can also be subsumed by a higher order or upper level factor, meaning that the higher order factor is defined by all the subordinate factors. Modeling the upper level factors requires them to be defined by all the information contained in all the subordinate factors. In other words, we can examine each subordinate factor independent of upper level factors, but upper level factors must contain all the subordinate factors.

Some researchers assume mistakenly that estimates of internal consistency, particularly Cronbach's alpha, can be used as evidence for item homogeneity or unidimensionality. This mistake results from the fact that reliability coefficients are only meaningful for unidimensional measures (Clark & Watson, 1995) and the fact that unidimensional constructs

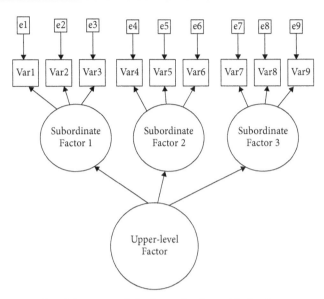

Figure 5.1 Graphical depiction of a higher order factor. [Online].
Available: https://web3.unt.edu/benchmarks/issues/2013/04/rss-matters.
Accessed December 8, 2013.

do yield high estimates of internal consistency (Green et al., 1977). Unfortunately, however, it is also easily possible to obtain a high measure of internal consistency in the absence of a common factor or among a set of heterogeneous items. This happens because estimates of internal consistency are based on correlations, and all kinds of variables correlate for many different reasons, one of which is their common dependence on a single factor. In addition, estimates of internal consistency increase with the addition of more items, with the number of redundant items, and with larger correlation coefficients. Any set of positively correlated items can yield an adequate estimate of internal consistency.

It is generally accepted in social work research that the items of a measure have moderate to high intercorrelations, thereby producing a high estimate of internal consistency. As mentioned earlier, a value of .70 is commonly used as an acceptable cutoff point. We also noted earlier that researchers should be cautious of such cutoffs, because there are theoretical considerations for both low and high interitem correlations. For example, Kline (1979) notes that intercorrelations less than .30 suggest that each part of the measure is measuring something different, whereas higher correlations (e.g., more than .80) may suggest the measure is too narrow and specific. Cattell (1978) argues further that researchers should avoid too high of item homogeneity because it results in bloated specific factors based on conceptually redundant items, which yields high internal consistency but erodes the validity of the measure. From this perspective, moderate to low item homogeneity is preferable to ensure that distinct facets of the construct are being represented.

Hattie (1985) summarizes different methods for examining the dimensionality of items, including indices based on answer patterns, principal components, factor analyses, and latent-trait analysis. Each method has its own unique set of strengths and weaknesses. CFA and IRT are the closest thing we have to a gold standard for testing item dimensionality (Netemeyer, Bearden, and Sharma, 2003; Raykov & Marcoulides, 2011). IRT, developed in the measurement of abilities, is rarely used in social work research. We recommend researchers begin with a thorough conceptual review of the construct and all existing measures of the construct, move into empirical item analyses, and end with a CFA based on a large sample.

A conceptual review involves careful examination of each item and its relationship with the target construct. This review requires the boundaries of the target construct to be adequately defined, especially when dealing with complex constructs. All facets of a target construct should be covered by the items. After a careful conceptual review, empirical work helps confirm hypotheses from the review regarding item appropriateness and characteristics, and typically involves examining the individual distributions of each item to identify potential problems such as floor or ceiling effects. Then, item correlations are examined. As mentioned, according to Kline (1979), we would seek a range of item correlations from .30 to .70 to facilitate adequate homogeneity and to ensure the coverage is not too broad or overly specific. Last, formal tests of dimensionality require the use of CFA, preferably with tests of alternative model specifications. For example, a unidimensional model should be compared directly with a multidimensional model.

Reflective and Formative Models

A critical and often misunderstood aspect of latent variables revolves around the theoretical distinction of whether the manifest variables are *reflections* or *causes* of change in the latent variable. The critical nature of this distinction is depicted graphically in Figure 5.2, which includes path diagrams used to represent latent-variable models. The ovals represent the latent variables, squares represent manifest variables, long single-headed arrows represent causal relationships, and double-headed arrows represent correlational relationships. The short single-headed arrows pointing to the indicators in Figure 5.2A and the small arrow pointing to the latent variable in Figure 5.2B represent measurement error.

The reflective model implies the latent variable gives rise to uniform and corresponding changes in the manifest variables. In other words, the manifest variables *reflect* changes in the latent variable, making the latent variable the *common cause* to all the manifest variables. A uniform change refers to the magnitude and the consistency in the direction of the association between the latent variable and the measured variables. That is, if the level of the latent variable increases, then as a consequence each of the manifest variables also increases. If the latent variable decreases, then for the same reason the manifest variables decrease. The manifest variables move in response to changes in the latent variable to the degree that their relationships with the latent variable are significantly stronger than their relationships with the error components, which are conceptualized as unknown (residual) latent variables.

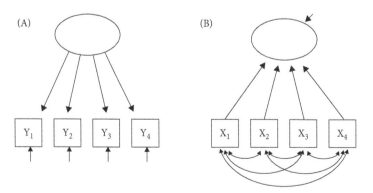

Figure 5.2 Graphical depiction of reflective and formative indicator models. (A) The reflective indicator model. (B) The formative indicator model.

As an example, the Beck Depression Inventory-II (see Beck et al., 1996) is a 21-item measure of depression. Depression is the latent variable and the 21 items are the manifest variables. The assumption of the Beck Depression Inventory-II, in addition to virtually all other latent variables in social work research, is that the manifest variables are reflective indicators, which assumes that any change in depression results in a uniform change to the manifest variables. In other words, changes in depression give rise to corresponding changes in all 21 manifest variables. Thus, depression is considered a *common cause* of the manifest variables.

Formative models, on the other hand, reverse the causal direction between the manifest variables and the latent variable. The manifest variables *determine* the latent variable, with changes in the latent variable resulting from changes in the manifest variables. This simple change in causal direction has huge theoretical implications. In direct contrast to the reflective model, the formative model does not imply uniformity or consistency among the manifest variables. Instead, the manifest variables may be correlated positively, negatively, or with a mixed pattern. Because the manifest variables are exogenous—that is, they do not regress on other variables—they are assumed to have been measured without error. This means the measurement error associated with the manifest variables becomes associated with the latent variable. It should be noted that exogenous variables are identified easily in graphic depictions of structural equation models because these variables have only a single-headed arrow emanating from the variable itself and pointing to another variable. In formative models, the set of manifest variables defines the latent variable. Deleting even one of the manifest variables changes the meaning of the latent variable.

As an example, consider socioeconomic status. Assume that the measured variables for socioeconomic status are current income, overall assets, education level, and occupation. In our example, these measured variables define or determine socioeconomic status. In other words, a change in one of the measured variables causes a change in the level of the latent variable. For example, a significant increase in current income level may occur, which gives rise to change in socioeconomic status. We may see a change in the level of assets with a significant change in current income, although this likely to be a delayed, because it may take time for assets to accumulate or to deplete. It may be possible that occupation has changed, but it is unlikely that the level of education would change.

Each one of the measured variables is a necessary component of socioeconomic status as defined in this model. Assets could not be excluded from the model or replaced with a different measured variable and still measure the same idea of socioeconomic status. Because of the direction of the causal relationships between the measured variables and latent construct, it would not make sense theoretically to claim changes in socioeconomic status give rise to uniform and consistent changes in the noted measured variables. Clearly, in the case of socioeconomic status, the process works the other way around.

It is helpful to engage in a series of thought experiments to establish appropriate causal hypotheses between latent and manifest variables. That is, it is important to ask whether the latent variable is a *common cause* of the manifest variables. If the latent variable is a common cause, then a change in the latent variable results in a uniform change among all the manifest variables. In the reflective model, the manifest variables are interchangeable, so deleting one of the manifest variables or adding a new one does not change the meaning of the latent variable. However, if these conditions do not hold, the construct in mind may be formative in nature.

If the target construct is formative, it is necessary to use a formative model. Because formative models are problematic in several ways, some researchers use reflective models more or less mindlessly. Interestingly, empirical results from an isolated formative model and an isolated reflective model of the same construct with the same set of manifest variables are similar. But, as soon as the research moves beyond tests of the isolated construct to testing hypotheses in the broader nomological net (Cronbach & Meehl, 1955), anomalies and inconsistencies show up. A consistent correspondence between the theoretical conception and latent variable is fundamental and critical.

In the next section, we discuss the actual strategies for the analysis of latent variables. However, we should note that all mainstream analytic procedures are for reflective indicator models. Procedures are not well established for analyzing latent variables specified as formative models. In fact, some researchers have argued that formative models should not be used at all (see Howell, 2008). Others have suggested respecifying formative models as reflective models. For example, socioeconomic status may be conceptualized as a reflective model with indicators such as: How high do you feel you are on the social ladder? (Borsboom, Mellenbergh, & van Heerden, 2004). Although some options exist for the analysis of formative models (e.g., multiple indicator, multiple cause models; partial least squares), they have their own limitations and are not common in social work research or other fields of study. Thus, we limit the following discussion of analytic strategies to reflective models but encourage those of you who are interested in specifying and analyzing formative models to consult the works of Diamantopoulos and Winklhofer (2001); Diamantopoulos, Riefler, and Roth (2008); Diamantopoulos and Siguaw (2006); and Jarvis, MacKenzie, and Podsakoff (2003).

Local Independence

An important assumption of reflective indicator models is that of *local independence,* which is actually an assumption that holds true across the full range of procedures for empirically testing latent-variable models. Local independence is a matter that is understood through a theoretical and conceptual assessment, as opposed to a statistical test. More specifically, we have already discussed in detail the important causal linkage that must exist between the latent variable and the indicators in the reflective indicator model. The causal linkage must be specified accurately according to theory. Regarding the assumption of local independence, there should be no causal associations among the indicators that are related causally to the latent variable. This is ultimately a theoretical assumption, because correlations exist by having the shared relationship with the latent variable. In other words, we would expect the indicators to move in unison with changes in the latent variable, but this movement should not be the result of any causal influences occurring between the indicators.

As an example, let's use depression as a latent variable measured using the following three supposed reflective indicators:

- disrupted sleep
- low mood or energy
- excess or lack of appetite

In this measurement model, we assume the latent variable depression gives rise to changes in all three of these indicators. The local independence assumption implies that a uniform change is explained wholly by the latent variable, and the correlations observed among the indicators are really spurious. The notion of local independence may be a very strong assumption being made in many measurement contexts, and is especially true with these indicators of depression. More specifically, working from the assumption of local independence, we assume that low mood or energy is not a result of disrupted sleep or dysregulated eating. Again, with such a measurement model, depression would account for each of the measured problems, as opposed to the measured problems having directional or reciprocal influences among themselves.

Analysis of Latent Variables

We define latent variables as a part of theory, and our analytic procedures are tools for deriving empirical evidence to refine our definitions and to test theory. When we talk about a latent-variable *model*, we are referring to the technical specification of the latent variable within an analytic framework. That is, our theory defines what the latent variable *is*, and the analytic strategy provides a *model* of that variable. Thus, we have a theoretical definition of the latent variable, and the *measurement model* of that latent variable serves as the crucial link between our data and theory. We have different analytic strategies based on the type of data of the observed or manifest variables and the level of measurement of our latent variable. It should be emphasized that the level of measurement of our observed and latent variables is always to be informed by theory, as opposed to what is convenient or most amenable to analysis.

Table 5.1 provides an overview of the major types of strategies for the analysis of latent variable models. We describe the major uses of each strategy, along with the levels of measurement for the observed and latent variable. All the analyses described next are for reflective indicator models. As stated previously, our statistical software has no capability to differentiate the actual direction of causality between the manifest variables and the latent variable, which is why it is crucial all the analyses be grounded in theory.

Factor Analysis

Exploratory Factor Analysis

EFA was the first strategy for analyzing latent-variable models. The primary data type involves continuous manifest variables, although methods have been developed for analyzing other types of variables (e.g.,

Table 5.1 Types of Latent-Variable Modeling Strategies and Their
Levels of Measurement

Analytic strategy	Level of measurement of indicators	Level of measurement of latent variable	Use
Exploratory factor analysis	Continuous or dichotomous	Continuous	Data reduction, exploration; often atheoretical
Confirmatory factor analysis	Continuous or dichotomous	Continuous	Hypothesis testing, theory based
Mixture model/ latent profile analysis	Continuous	Categorical	Subgroup inference from data
Latent class analysis	Categorical	Categorical	Subgroup inference from data

dichotomous indicators). The latent variable is almost always specified at the continuous or interval level. Researchers commonly use EFA in two different ways: to *explore* or *discover* latent variables within a set of indicators and to *explore* or *discover* the structure or dimensions (also referred to as *subscales* or *factors*) of a latent variable. Although some methods have been devised for using EFA techniques to test hypothesized structures, the application of EFA in social work research is almost always exploratory.

Many social work researchers overextend their interpretation of EFA results by claiming the results provide evidence for validity and reliability. It is important to keep in mind that, assuming basic requirements are met for conducting an EFA, at least one factor will always be extracted, and the exclusion of any indicator can produce an entirely different factor structure. For these reasons, researchers should not consider the results of EFA alone as evidence of either validity or reliability. EFA should be used as a hypothesis-generating tool. Although EFA can be used to test a hypothesized factor structure, this hypothesis-testing procedure is done more effectively with CFA.

Confirmatory Factor Analysis
CFA is a technique of SEM and it represents a major advancement in measurement. Although EFA is designed for exploring hypothesized

factor structures, CFA provides explicit tests of hypothesized structures. Researchers make a priori specifications of which manifest variables or indicators are associated with the latent variable. A variety of fit indices are used to help describe the empirical correspondence between the model and the data.

Most statistical programs also provide modification indices to indicate how changes to the model can improve fit. A serious mistake researchers make is to use the modification indices to make changes to the model and then to reanalyze the model with the same data. The modification indices are completely naive to theory. Because the model itself is a representation of theory, researchers who engage in this practice are, ultimately, letting the statistical software determine theoretical changes. Moreover, using the same data simply capitalizes on chance variation in the data; it is unlikely the results will be stable across new data. We recommend that modification indices be used to help researchers think comprehensively about possible reasons why the model failed to exhibit a good fit with the data.

Latent Class and Profile Analysis

Latent class and profile analysis are very similar to factor analysis. In general, latent class analysis involves dichotomous indicators whereas latent profile analysis involves continuous indicators. Recent advancements in software allow for increased ease of modeling of these different indicators. For these analyses the latent variable is categorical, reflecting subgroups or classes within the sample. More specifically, consider the measurement of depression. From a factor analytic standpoint, we measure a latent variable to reflect different levels of depression in the sample. We order persons on a latent continuum from low to high levels of depression, and indicate a particular place on the scale. This measurement approach follows the logic of the reflective model approach, in which an underlying latent variable gives rise to changes in placement of this continuum. The logic for latent class and profile analysis is the same, although the underlying latent variable gives rise to qualitative differences in the expression of depression. The goal is to establish a set of categories or groups of respondents that share the same expression of symptoms as other persons in that category.

The application of latent class and profile analysis in social work research is very similar to that of EFA. That is, a researcher uses this analytic strategy as an exploratory tool, looking to discover different possible latent class or profile models that exist in a sample. A series of different models is considered, typically starting with a single group and then assessing the fit when additional groups are added to the model. The researcher selects the model with the *best* fit, which is based on empirical indices of fit and conceptual plausibility. The empirical fit indices appear straightforward, because various guidelines exist to determine which model has the best fit. However, significant debate exists regarding thresholds for acceptable levels and how they should be interpreted.

Conceptual plausibility is more difficult to assess because the initial analysis was largely *atheoretical*. Conceptual plausibility needs to have some empirical support by correlating the model with other variables thought to be correlated. But, the valence, or direction of effects, is not as straightforward as the factor analytic model because the different groups can be associated with measures that have different levels of effects and magnitudes of differences. The theory required to specify hypotheses with such precision would have to be very specific and rigorous, and in social work research this is rarely the case.

Confirmatory approaches are possible with latent class and profile analysis. However, as stated previously, these approaches are rare and require a significant amount of theory to make specifications of the model. The specifications of the model largely assume the number of classes identified, but no specification to the level or probability of the indicators for each group and the expected class sizes is given. Thus, a priori specification represents an overall structure as opposed to the actual composition of the model.

LATENT-VARIABLE MODELS AND VALIDITY EVIDENCE

EFA and CFA are the primary analytic strategies for examining the structure of latent variables. The underlying mathematics of these models is based on linear and matrix algebra. The end result of factor analyses produces information on the correlation structure among a set of observed variables. The inferences we make from the results are ultimately grounded in the underlying theory of the construct. In this section, we review the types of validity evidence that can be derived from latent-variable factor models, with a distinction between the results of EFA and CFA. Then, we consider more broadly the interpretation of results and how they bear on the underlying theory of the measure. As noted by Thompson and Daniel (1996), factor analysis and construct validity have often been associated with each other. For example, Nunnally (1978) spoke of factorial validity, arguing that "[f]actor analysis is at the heart of the measurement of psychological constructs" (as cited in Thompson and Daniel [1996, p. 198]). Such views have led researchers to think that analytic strategies can be used to define scientific constructs and theories, which is never the case (Thompson & Daniel, 1996; Mulaik, 1994). Factor analysis can contribute preliminary evidence for the validity of a construct, referred to as "trait validity" by Campbell (1960), but factor analytic results of a measurement model alone do not yield evidence of construct validity or what Campbell called "nomological validity." Factor analysis can be used to help test and inform the refinement of theories, but the validity evidence ultimately necessitates sound theory. Social work researchers must remain extremely cautious of the allure of using factor analytic strategies for defining and discovering new constructs.

We have two major types of factor analysis: EFA and CFA. EFA is used for discovering possible theoretical structures or patterns among a set of observed variables. This procedure is typically implemented when a researcher has no a priori hypothesis about the structure of the data or possible patterns. CFA, which is a type of SEM, requires a researcher to specify and test a hypothesized correlational structure or pattern among a set of manifest variables. It should be noted that EFA could be used to test hypothesized structures, but this is not what it was designed for and more information is given through CFA. CFA is the dominant and preferred approach to hypothesis testing.

Although we believe that EFA has utility for generating testable hypotheses that can lead to the creation or refinement of theory, exploratory evidence is *not* validity evidence. In fact, as long as some basic data requirements are met, at least one factor—even a completely nonsensical factor from nonsensical data—can be extracted. Thus, EFA results need to be subjected to hypothesis testing, which is done via CFA. But, again, we emphasize that even the results of a single-factor CFA do not provide construct validity evidence. The results of a CFA need to be considered in context of the underlying theory.

The fit of a particular model and what to do with the results is complex. Other texts provide ways of assessing model fit (Kline, 2010). Of course, we can have varying levels of fit, and the litmus for determining what is and is not acceptable can differ across studies. To facilitate clarity, we limit our discussion to these two broad categories—acceptable versus not acceptable—and consider how decisions have important consequences with respect to validity.

Researchers too often assume that acceptable model fit, based on model fit indices, is sufficient validity evidence for a given construct. Although the results may contribute to the overall body of validity evidence, it is not comprehensive nor is it sufficient. A number of other factors deserve careful consideration—most notably, theory. More specifically, it is relatively easy to construct a measure that has modest correspondence with theory, collect some data that are subjected to factor analytic procedures, and obtain results that suggest a *good fit*. For example, a measure of socioeconomic status specified as a formative model but analyzed within a factor analytic framework (i.e., a reflective model) can still produce evidence of a good fit. However, computer programs that implement factor analytic procedures have no way of telling the researcher whether the causal associations between the observed and latent variables are specified correctly or incorrectly. Thus, it is essential that every factor analytic model is first assessed according to theory before looking at fit statistics.

Another important consideration is that numerous other alternative models based on the same data can be specified and also exhibit a good fit with the data. Thus, it is important to specify and test alternative models and to interpret results in the context of theory. Alternative models that exhibit a good fit with the data could be interpreted rightfully as evidence that the underlying theory is ambiguous and needs further specification.

A model that does not exhibit a good fit with the data obviously cannot provide validity evidence. The complication that follows an unacceptable model fit is discerning the actual source of the problem. Researchers must be cautious of assuming problems with the measure itself and making modifications to the model or the measure. Many models exhibit a poor fit with the data. A number of possible explanations exist, and it is important that all possibilities be given careful consideration before making modifications to the measure, particularly modifications based on use of modification indices that available in all software packages that implement CFA. For example, the measure itself could have a technical flaw that contributes to a poor fit, which would justify a modification to the measure. But, equally plausible explanations exist, including an improperly specified theory, poor correspondence between the theory and the measure, causal heterogeneity in the sample, and failure to meet assumptions of multivariate normality.

Issues of causal heterogeneity typically occur when researchers fail to consider the generalizability of the causal processes being studied. More specifically, a measure of depression may be constructed for a western or English–speaking sample but administered to a culturally diverse sample. The actual interpretation of the items and their theoretical linkage to the latent variable may not be consistent. For example, an item that has often been used as an indicator of depression is "feeling blue." Although *feeling blue* may be readily understood by native English speakers, it does not have a direct translation in other languages.

RELIABILITY AND LATENT-VARIABLE MODELS

Structural equation models in general and CFA specifically provide a way of examining reliability systematically. More specifically, the procedures of SEM allow the researcher to assess the reliability of each observed variable and to estimate theoretical and measurement parameters concomitantly. The potential for distortion in theoretical parameters is high when measurement error is ignored. In addition, the more complicated the model (e.g., large number of observed variables relative to the number of latent variables), the more important it becomes to take measurement error into account. At the same time, the overall fit of a structural equation model is based on all the parameters of the model. It is helpful to think about the number of relationships that are part of the measurement models of the structural equation model, and the number of structural relationships or the relationships between the latent variables. Although the structural equation model may be a test of the theory, the overall number of relationships in the measurement model may be determining the overall fit of the model. Thus, a strategy must be devised to establish reliability and validity evidence for a measure, but subsequently to reduce the overall number of indicators to test the theory effectively. This can be done using single-item measures or item parcels, although they have strengths and limitations that need to be considered.

Single-Item Measures

Single-item measures involve the measurement of a concept or construct with just one item or question. Single-item measures can reduce the burden on respondents or observers, and analyzing data from single items can be rather straightforward. As described by Rossiter (2002), the use of a single-item measure (as opposed to multiple items) is sufficient if the construct, as the respondent understands it, is *concrete singular*, meaning the object is imagined easily and uniformly. The other criterion required is that the attribute of the construct is concrete—again, imagined easily and uniformly (Bergkvist & Rossiter, 2007). For example, if research was being conducted with persons who have been long-term participants in Alcoholics Anonymous (AA), the concept of an AA meeting (object) is imagined easily and uniformly. If we were interested in measuring the sense of *community* in AA meetings, that attribute would likely be imagined easily, but it is unlikely that what is imagined would be consistent across the respondents, suggesting the need for multiple items for this particular attribute.

Keep in mind that the use of single items raises concerns about their reliability. In particular, we can have greater confidence in the reliability of multiple-item measures because we can compute correlations among items, which gives us an estimate of internal consistency. And, as described in detail by Bergkvist and Rossiter (2007), multiple items offer more information because they tap more facets of a given construct, whereas a single item offers a global rating only.

Whenever a single-item measure is used in a full structural equation model, it is necessary also to specify an estimate of its error (refer to the previous section on latent and manifest variables). The following two steps describe how to carry this out:

1. If a single parcel has been created based on a set of items, obtain the reliability estimate for the scale and use this value as an estimate of the unique variance for the indicator. If a reliability estimate cannot be derived from the existing data,

use the existing literature to obtain an approximate reliability estimate. If the literature fails to include any information on reliability, as might happen with a new measure, then—drawing clues from the theory or experience—estimate a theoretically possible high reliability estimate, a low estimate, and a median estimate. Differences in model results from the use of these three estimates provides useful information on the consequences of error in this particular measure.

2. Subtract the reliability estimate from one and then multiply that quantity with the sample variance of the scale: (1 – Reliability) × Sample variance. This computed value is used as a fixed parameter estimate. Although it does not estimate the unique variance for the measure, it avoids the assumption that the measure is without error (see Williams & O'Boyle, 2008).

ITEM PARCELS IN SEM

A full structural equation model takes into consideration the hypothesized relationships among a set of items with latent constructs, and hypothesized relationships among the latent constructs. Although it is desirable to incorporate measurement models in the full structural equation model, it may not be desirable to include all items from the original measurement model for a couple reasons. First, although no single sample size rule exists in the application of SEM, a sufficient sample size is typically justified based on the overall number of parameters in an estimated model. Thus, a structural equation model that incorporates all the items for each latent variable could easily result in a large number of parameters to be estimated, making it impractical to achieve an adequate sample (Williams & O'Boyle, 2008). The problem is compounded further because a large number of items contribute to a larger covariance matrix, making it less likely the model will fit the data even though it matches closely the processes and theoretical relationships under study (Williams & O'Boyle, 2008).

One of the most common methods to address this problem involves the use of item parcels—that is, a sum score of several items assessing the same unidimensional construct (Kishton & Widaman, 1994). The researcher must first establish the hypothesized structure using all the items in a CFA. Then, the use of item parcels must be justified clearly. In most cases, such a justification is clear when a single construct accounts for a disproportionate number of parameters being estimated. After parcels are created, this model should then be reexamined using CFA to ensure the hypothesized structure is maintained. See Kline (2010) for a further discussion of this topic.

Keep in mind that the use of item parcels does carry potential problems. For example, a loss of information is inherent in the use of item parcels because each item presumably contains unique information about what is rated. Of course, we are attempting to maximize the amount of information by selecting an appropriate parceling strategy (described later), but no item-parceling strategy can retain the full information. In other words, we can think of item parceling as a variable reduction strategy, because it attempts to reduce a large set of indicators to the smallest number possible while avoiding a loss of information. In addition, reliability that can be achieved through the use of multiple items can also be eroded during this process, given that higher estimates of reliability can be achieved through the use of multiple-item scales.

Williams and O'Boyle (2008) report various strategies that have been used in the management literature for creating item parcels.

- *Random assignment*: A number of parcels are determined a priori for the items, and each of the nine items are assigned randomly and without replacement to one of the parcels. For example, if we had a scale comprised of nine items, we could reduce it to three items using three separate parcels. Each parcel would be based on the information from the three items. The average of the item values in the parcel would be calculated and used in place of the three original item values. This approach should lead to roughly equal common factor variance across parcels. It works best when items are based on the same response scales and have similar variances (Williams & O'Boyle, 2008).
- *Item-to-construct balance*: This method of parceling attempts to balance items equally in terms of their difficulty and discrimination. A CFA with all items is first conducted. Standardized factor loadings from the model serve as a guide for item assignment. For example, three parcels may be created for a nine-item measure of a unidimensional construct. All nine

items are rank ordered in terms of their standardized factor loadings. The items with highest factor loading are assigned to the first parcel, the second highest are assigned to the second parcel, and the third highest to the third parcel. This process of assignment continues among the three parcels until all items have been assigned.

- *A priori questionnaire construction*: With this strategy, knowledge of the items is used during the construction of parcels. Items may be distributed among the parcels for reasons such as negative or positive wording. If this method is used, it is important to explicate the specific substantive rationale and process of item assignment.
- *Correlational algorithm*: This process is similar to the item-to-construct balance strategy. Instead of using standardized factor loadings, interitem correlations are used to assign items to parcels. Thus, the two items with the highest correlation are assigned to the first parcel, the two items with the next highest correlation are assigned to the second parcel, and so on.
- *Radial algorithm*: This strategy is a hybrid of the item-to-construct balance and the correlation algorithm. The first step involves examining all nine items with a CFA. Then, a pair of indicators is selected for each parcel. The pair of indicators selected is based on the smallest absolute difference between factor loadings. The unassigned items and the item parcels (comprised on the initial selection of item pairs) is then subject to another CFA, and the items are assigned to the parcels with the closest primary factor loading to their own (see Rogers & Schmitt, 2004).
- *Correlated uniqueness*: This strategy involves the use of modification indices for the creation of item parcels. That is, the items are examined to determine which items have uniqueness that covary. These items are then assigned to the same parcel.

We do not recommend any one of these strategies over another. Each strategy is reasonable. The question is what works best with the particular data and theory at hand. The selection of given strategy varies depending on the unique circumstances of the research being conducted. Thus, it is critical that researchers communicate clearly both how and why they created item parcels.

KEY POINTS

- Latent variables are unobserved variables inferred from hypothesized data patterns of manifest variables.
- We hypothesize the existence of latent variables because they help to reduce the complexity of data, simplify the testing of theory, and increase the accuracy of empirical results.
- Manifest variables are measured through one or more of the five human senses: sight, smell, taste, touch, and hearing.
- Perhaps the most basic distinction between manifest and latent variables is that all manifest variables include measurement error, whereas latent variables are typically measured without random measurement error.
- We use substantive theory to help determine the extent to which error-free inferences can be made from the data to the variable structure.
- We incorporate measurement error explicitly when a manifest variable is used in place of or as a reference to a latent variable.
- To order people based on a specified attribute, observe individual differences, create groups, and establish meaningful associations among variables, it is necessary that the variables be unidimensional.
- Reflective indicator models assume changes in the latent variable and give rise to uniform changes in the manifest variables.
- Formative models assume measured variables define the latent variable.
- We must discern clearly whether each construct we are measuring implies a reflective model or formative model. Substantive theory, not data analysis, establishes the direction of causality between the measured variables and latent variable.
- Common latent-variable modeling procedures (Table 5.1) are not appropriate for formative models. The most efficient way to use a formative construct is to include it in a larger nomological net of constructs based on reflective models.
- EFA is used for discovering possible theoretical structures or patterns among a set of observed variables. This procedure is typically implemented when a researcher has no a priori hypothesis about the structure of the data or possible patterns.

- CFA requires a researcher to specify and test a hypothesized correlational structure or pattern among a set of manifest variables. CFA provides a strategy for generating preliminary validity evidence for a latent variable whereas EFA does not.
- Item parcels can be used to reduce the number of indicators that comprise a latent variable, but they do have threats to validity and reliability.

RECOMMENDED AND CLASSIC READINGS

Bollen, K.A. 1998. Structural equation models. In P. Armitage and T. Colton (Eds), *Encyclopedia of biostatistics* (pp. 4363–4372). Sussex, England: John Wiley.

Bollen, K., & Lennox, R. (1991). Conventional wisdom on measurement: A structural equation perspective. *Psychological Bulletin, 110*(2), 305–314. [Note: This is a classic article that provides important information on latent-variable models, particularly in making distinctions between formative and reflective indicators, as well as the (im)proper usage of Cronbach's alpha.]

Borsboom, D. (2008). Latent variable theory. *Measurement, 6*, 25–53.

Bryant, F. B., & Yarnold, P. R. (1995). Principal-components analysis and confirmatory factor analysis. In L. G. Grimm & P. R. Yarnold (Eds.), *Reading and understanding multivariate statistics* (pp. 99–136). Washington, DC: American Psychological Association.

Cattell, R. B. (1978). *Scientific use of factor analysis in behavioral and life sciences.* New York: Plenum.

Diamantopoulos, A., & Winklhofer, H. M. (2001). Index construction with formative indicators: An alternative to scale development. *Journal of Marketing Research, 38*(2), 269–277.

Fabrigar, L. R., Wegener, D. T., MacCallum, R. C., & Strahan, E. J. (1999). Evaluating the use of exploratory factor analysis in psychological research. *Psychological Methods, 4*(3), 272–299.

Gorsuch, R. L. (1997). Exploratory factor analysis: Its role in item analysis. *Journal of Personality Assessment, 68*(3), 532–560.

Jöreskog, K. G., & Goldberger, A. S. (1975). Estimation of a model with multiple indicators and multiple causes of a single latent variable. *Journal of the American Statistical Association, 70*(351A), 631–639.

Kishton, J. M., & Widaman, K. F. (1994). Unidimensional versus domain representative parceling of questionnaire items: An empirical example. *Education and Psychological Measurement, 54*(3), 757–765.

Kline, R. B. (2010). *Principles and practice of structural equation modeling.* New York: Guilford Press.

Linn, R. L. (1990). Has item response theory increased the validity of achievement test scores? *Applied Measurement in Education, 3*(2), 115–141.

Marsh, H. W., Balla, J. R., & McDonald, R. P. (1988). Goodness-of-fit indexes in confirmatory factor analysis: The effect of sample size. *Psychological Bulletin, 103*(3), 391–410.

Raykov, T. (2000). On sensitivity of structural equation modeling to latent relation misspecifications. *Structural Equation Modeling, 7*(4), 596–607.

Williams, L. J., & O'Boyle, E. H. (2008). Measurement models for linking latent variables and indicators: A review of human resource management research using parcels. *Human Resource Management Review, 18*, 233–242.

6

Writing and Reviewing Measurement Studies

I believe in evidence. I believe in observation, measurement, and reasoning, confirmed by independent observers. I'll believe anything, no matter how wild and ridiculous, if there is evidence for it. The wilder and more ridiculous something is, however, the firmer and more solid the evidence will have to be.

—Isaac Asimov

A variety of resources exist that guide researchers on the empirical aspects of measurement issues, with a focus on factor analysis (e.g., Cabrera-Nguyen, 2010; Worthington & Whittaker, 2006). These resources are helpful for promoting rigorous research and consistency in use and interpretation, and helping ensure consistency among reviewers in the peer review process. One limitation of these resources is the minimal attention given to the theoretical and conceptual issues that must be fully considered and appreciated before we can make substantive interpretations of empirical results.

The purpose of this chapter is to fill this gap in practical resources by offering both authors and reviewers suggestions for thinking about key theoretical and conceptual issues in measurement. We divide this chapter into two parts. The first part contains a few guiding principles we believe are necessary in advancing the field's thinking about measurement issues. We consider these *guiding principles* because they do not prescribe or proscribe any particular action. Rather, they are intended to serve as a lens for thinking about key measurement issues that are often problematic in social work publications.

The second part of this chapter presents a set of strategies to improve measurement reporting practices in social work research. These strategies are much more specific than the guiding principles. It is important to acknowledge that neither the guiding principles nor the specific strategies are comprehensive, and their relevance may vary by different areas of study within social work research. Nonetheless, we are confident they are an important point of departure for elevating the significance of the theoretical and conceptual issues of measurement.

GUIDING PRINCIPLES FOR WRITING AND REVIEWING MANUSCRIPTS

Focus on Validity

As emphasized throughout this handbook, validity is the most important measurement issue. Thus, anything written about measurement should, in some way, relate back to validity. One way to achieve a focus on validity is to move beyond reviews of psychometric properties to making explicit statements that answer the question: What is the theory and evidence that justify the inferences from a given measurement? Furthermore, by focusing on validity more explicitly, researchers may soon discover important gaps in theory and evidence in the measurement strategies considered a gold standard in a particular area of study. This shift in focus can open up new opportunities for thoughtful critiques and interpretations of existing research, in addition to opening new avenues for future research.

Write to Promote Replication

Formal replication studies are not common to social work research, which is a serious problem, because replication is critical to the advancement of scientific knowledge (Freese, 2007; King, 1995). Writing manuscripts that allow for replication does not necessarily lead to replication studies, but doing so helps to ensure sufficient information is provided to help readers understand both the form and function of each measure. The significance of this guiding principle can be fully appreciated by recognizing how a small or simple change in measurement and its inferences can lead to fundamentally different data or interpretations of data. Writing for replication can also help ensure consistency in the use of both existing and newly constructed measures.

Avoid Biased Language

Any type of bias that finds its way into the scientific method can limit the advancement of scientific knowledge. Although we are unaware of any recent attempts to quantify this bias in the field of social work, it is unlikely that the bias in social work differs from the social science and allied health disciplines. A recent study by Fanelli (2010) found that "the odds of reporting a positive result were around 5 times higher among papers in the disciplines of Psychology, Psychiatry, Economics, and Business compared to Space Science, 2.3 times higher in the domain of social sciences compared to the physical sciences, and 3.4 times higher in studies applying behavioural and social methodologies on people compared to physical and chemical studies on non-biological material" (p. e10068). Those of you who are skeptical of this claim can likely find compelling anecdotal evidence of publication bias in social work journals simply by perusing any recent social work journal.

Prevention of bias is the most important and obvious step in reducing bias. It may come as a surprise that publication bias originates with researchers—not journal editors (Dickersin, Min, & Meinert, 1992). Within the context of negative findings, researchers choose not to submit their research. A problem related to publication bias is the tendency for researchers to oversell their research, particularly in the context of measurement. Although we have not investigated this problem systematically, it is easy to spot uses of adjectives and other communication devices to influence readers' impression about a selected measurement strategy.

The following quotes are examples from the methods sections of recent social work publications. We have purposefully excluded the specific references to these examples and have slightly altered the phrasing to ensure we do not criticize any particular researcher, given that the examples appear to be representative of broader practices in the field. Italics have been added for emphasis.

- "This measure is considered the *gold standard.. ..*"
  Comment: The characterization of a measure as a gold standard approach usually means it is the most common and accepted measurement strategy. We encourage both authors and reviewers to remain skeptical of claims regarding gold standards that are not made in the context of validity. Arguments for a gold standard are fundamentally different than arguments for validity.
- "Previous research has *validated* this measure.. .."
  Comment: This is one of the more serious and problematic claims about measurement. Foremost, it suggests that validity is a static state when, in fact, it is continually evolving. Although validity evidence from prior research is important, this evidence cannot generalize to all subsequent uses of the same measure. It is important researchers see validity evidence at all stages of a research program.
- "Our selected measures have *excellent psychometric.. ..*"
  Comment: Although earlier conceptualizations of measurement may regard validity and reliability to be properties of a measure, it is important to recognize how and why this is inconsistent with contemporary validity theory. Keep in mind that psychometric evidence should, in some way, relate back to the inferences being made from a measure.
- "*High levels* of internal consistency (Cronbach's alpha >.90) provide *strong evidence* of reliability.. .."
  Comment: Be cautious in characterizing any single statistic as being strong evidence of reliability—especially validity. No single statistic can serve as the foundation for either reliability or validity arguments.

Make Substantive Interpretations of Statistics

Perhaps one of the most problematic issues limiting the advancement of measurement in social work research is our overreliance on arbitrary statistical thresholds and conventions. The overvaluation of the threshold $p < .05$

has been heavily criticized (see Cohen, 1994), although it is a threshold that maintains prominence in social work research. In the context of measurement, Cronbach's alpha serves an excellent illuminating example, with the widespread belief that higher alpha values are more desirable than lower alpha values. Thus, researchers actively seek high correlations, without considering the point of diminishing return.

To illustrate this problem, we can readily agree that a low Cronbach's alpha value indicates low levels of internal consistency, and higher values obviously indicate higher levels of internal consistency. But, consider for a moment what it actually means if we observe values that approach 1.0 (e.g., .9999). This means complete redundancy among the measure items. So, the question becomes: How high is too high for Cronbach's alpha? We can also extend this same logic when we are looking at convergent evidence in validity analyses. In other words, high values can be just as problematic as low values, but in much different ways. Whether we are seeking evidence for validity or reliability, we argue that a best practice in measurement involves making substantive interpretations of all statistics while avoiding the illusion that thresholds and conventions will pave the path to methodological and theoretical rigor.

Seek Construct Clarity

The quality of measurement is dependent on the clarity of our constructs. As described by Suddaby (2010), construct clarity is different than construct validity, and many scientific papers have faced rejection simply because of the lack of construct clarity. That is, authors have fallen short in the use of clear and accurate terms to ensure constructs are defined crisply and precisely. Suddaby (2010) argues that authors can improve the definitional clarity of constructs by doing the following:

1. Use language carefully to create precise categorical distinctions between concepts.
2. Delineate the conditions or circumstances under which a construct does or does not apply.
3. Provide clear conceptual distinctions and highlight semantic relationships to other related constructs.
4. Demonstrate coherence or logical consistency of the construct in relation to the overall theoretical argument being made.

IMPROVING MEASUREMENT REPORTING PRACTICES

The previous section reviews what we consider to be important guiding principles with respect to measurement in social work research. This list can certainly be expanded, but for purposes of brevity we believe it is an excellent point of departure. Along with these guiding principles, we highlight in the following pages a variety of ways that measurement reporting practices can be improved in your own research. Our recommended practices are based on many of the problems we have observed in social work research, and the regular problems we ask authors to resolve during the peer review process. We organize these recommendations based on the headings of a standard scientific paper.

Introduction (I)

Determine the Role of Measurement When Reviewing Empirical Evidence (I1)

The purpose of an introduction in scientific research is to provide readers with a background of scientific studies of what is known and unknown about a particular phenomenon to help readers understand how the current study bridges this gap in knowledge. Our scientific knowledge of concepts within the social and psychological worlds can be understood and advanced only through sound measurement practices. Thus, it behooves authors to discuss current knowledge and the desired level and kind of knowledge in the context of measurement.

Recognize That Precedent in Measurement Can Be (and Often Is) Wrong (I2)

As Kuhn (1962) argued in his highly influential book *The Structure of Scientific Revolutions,* normal periods of scientific development are driven by paradigms. The role of paradigms is to supply scientists with puzzles to be solved and tools for solving them. Among the most important tools in social work research is measurement. Often, the precedents for measurement are established, making it difficult to see how a widely established precedent may be problematic. Be sure to look comprehensively and critically at existing measurement strategies, particularly if they appear to be serving as a precedent. All precedents are worth revisiting, because scientific advancements may be limited by our measurement strategies.

Methods (M)

Relate Everything Written Back to Validity Everything Written about Measurement Should, in Some Way, Relate Back to Validity (M1)

Although this proviso is a reiteration of a guiding measurement principle, the redundancy is warranted. Again, the most important concern in measurement is validity, so all the measurement descriptions must, in some way, contribute to the understanding of validity. Keeping this in mind, the following strategies will be helpful.

Describe Specific Rules Used in Variable Construction (M2)

Many of the variables we examine in social work research use multiple indicators. It is critical that readers have clarity on how the indicators are scored and combined. It is often the case that indicators are simply added to create an overall score or a subscale score. Be sure readers know the specific procedures used for constructing any score used in the study. Furthermore, it is necessary to inform readers whether indicators were dropped from the final score and, if so, the rationale for those decisions.

Provide Conceptual Definitions for Study Variables (M3)

When using standardized or existing measures, it is important to provide clear conceptual definitions of the concepts being measured. For example, the study may use a measure of social capital and may indicate it was measured by a particular standardized measure. However, readers must still be provided with a clear conceptual definition for the concept, as opposed simply to naming the measure.

Provide Comprehensive Measurement Descriptions for Key Independent and Dependent Variables (M4)

A challenge that authors routinely experience is finding a balance between breadth and depth in measurement descriptions. That is, most journals have very strict page limits or word counts, which necessarily reduce the amount of information that can be included in a manuscript. It may be difficult or even impossible to provide comprehensive validity arguments for each measure. A more practical approach involves identifying what are regarded as the key independent and dependent variables, and ensuring those variables are given the most attention in the manuscript. What is considered *key* is obviously subjective, but the most practical way of addressing this issue is starting with the study hypotheses.

*Give Examples of Items When Using Scales That Are
Relatively Unknown (M5)*

Social work research is continually adding new measures to its existing
base of knowledge, and many of these measures are relatively unknown
to other researchers. When using a scale that is new or not commonly
used, be sure to provide a few specific examples of the items (see Kashy,
Donnellan, Ackerman, & Russell, 2009).

Ensure Clarity between Validity Evidence and Reliability Evidence (M6)

Be cautious of reviewing evidence under the generic category of psychometrics. Validity and reliability have very important relationships to
each other, but they serve very different roles during the research process. Whenever possible, describe validity and reliability separately, and
then provide bridging statements that show how they are relate to each
other with respect to the inferences being made.

*Identify the Types of Validity and Reliability Evidence That Have Not
Been Collected and Describe the Implications for Interpreting the
Current and Future Research (M7)*

Chapters 3 and 4 review different types of evidence for validity and
reliability. Although some of the distinctions between the different
types can be small, the differences are very important. Thus, it is helpful to readers to ensure the differences are made clear. When reviewing evidence for validity and reliability, review the evidence that is
available, but also identify the types of evidence that have not yet been
gathered.

*Provide Rationales and Substantive Interpretations for
All Constructed or Transformed Measures (M8)*

Constructing measures and transforming measures (e.g., dichotomiz-
ing an interval-level variable) is not an uncommon practice in social
work research. Unfortunately, providing a sound rationale and substantive interpretation of each measure and transformed measure is
uncommon. It is important to highlight the problem being solved.
At the same time, you should not forget that it is often the case that
addressing one problem creates another problem. For example, dichot-
omizing a variable results in a significant loss of statistical power.
Furthermore, moving too quickly to the process used to construct the

measures and transform them prevents you from thinking about the source of the problem.

Justify the Use of Any Analytic Strategy for Constructing or Investigating a Measure (M9)

With the development of user-friendly statistical software, social work researchers can use more easily a wide range of analytic tools for constructing and investigating measures. It is important, in particular, with respect to latent-variable modeling, that a clear justification or rationale be provided for the use of any given analytic strategy. Every strategy has particular assumptions that have implications for validity. Make these assumptions and implications part of the justification.

Results

Provide Univariate Summaries of All Study Variables (R1)

For readers to have a comprehensive understanding of the measures, present univariate statistics for all study variables before relating them to each other in more complex correlational analyses. Doing so allows readers to make independent assessments with respect to the distribution of the data.

Use Current Data as Sources of Validity and Reliability Evidence Whenever Possible (R2)

As discussed in earlier chapters, validity and reliability evidence represents properties of data, not properties of a measure. Thus, it is important that evidence for validity and reliability be supplied for the current study data whenever possible. Although a prior estimate of reliability or validity may be useful, it is certainly less useful than estimates derived from the current data source.

Include a Table of Correlations When Multiple Outcome Variables Are Assessed (R3)

A table of correlations is necessary to help readers understand the possible redundancy present among multiple outcome variables. As suggested by Kashy et al. (2009), when large differences in the group means are observed, partial correlations can be computed, controlling for the effects of independent variables.

Discussion

*Maintain Consistency with the Conceptual Definitions and
Levels of Measurement (D1)*
Scientific discussions provide a great degree of scholarly freedom with
respect to interpretation and speculation. However, it is important that
consistency in the conceptual definitions and levels of measurement be
maintained. For example, measurement of worker burnout symptoms
and depressive symptoms (interval-level measurement) is not the same
as the measurement of burnout and depression (nominal-level measurement), although we often take liberty in extending our conceptual definition beyond its original conceptual bounds.

*Avoid Generalities When Making Recommendations for
Improving Measures (D2)*
The advancement of measurement is among the most important factors in the advancement of scientific knowledge. Thus, it makes sense
that discussion sections include critiques of measurement. We recommend this practice with the proviso that recommendations specifically
address what needs to be improved. Keep in mind that the recommendations ultimately need to speak to validity.

*Avoid Post Hoc Critiques of Measurement in the Context of
Negative Findings (D3)*
Although we believe it is good practice to consider the role of measurement in the interpretation of study findings, we also encourage
researchers to avoid post hoc critiques when study findings do not provide support for the study hypotheses. In particular, most critiques of
measurement can be done easily before a study or a particular analysis
is conducted. If the measurement is a weak link in the study, this should
be identified before the analysis.

KEY POINTS

- Numerous sources offer standards or guidance with respect
  to the empirical aspects of measurement. This attention
  overshadows the complexities of the theoretical and conceptual
  aspects necessary for establishing the value of measurement.

- Validity is the most important aspect of measurement. Anything written about measurement should, in some way, relate back to validity.
- Writing to promote replication can help ensure the necessary details of measurement are communicated in a manuscript.
- We must ensure the distinction between validity and reliability is evident. Validity is not the same as reliability, and reliability is not the same as validity. Although this may seem self-evident, these concepts are often confused in the literature.
- We must try to strike a balance between being concise and being precise in measurement descriptions.

SUGGESTED READINGS

General Scientific Writing

The following articles serve as resources on scientific writing. Although they do not focus on measurement, these resources provide an important context for thinking about general writing strategies. For example, one common theme present throughout these resources is the importance of communicating ideas in the simplest way possible, without actually oversimplifying the ideas. Measurement is complicated, and it is important to think about how to convey measurement-related information in a relatively simple way while avoiding the problem of oversimplification. This is one of many examples of how critical thinking and writing can help advance the practice of measurement.

Alley, M., & Sestak, Z. (1996). *The craft of scientific writing*. New York: Springer.

Gopen, G., & Swan, J. (1990). The science of scientific writing: If the reader is to grasp what the writer means, the writer must understand what the reader needs. *American Scientist, 78*(6), 550–558.

Holmes, F. L. (1987). Scientific writing and scientific discovery. *Isis, 78*(2), 220–235.

Kashy, D. A., Donnellan, M. B., Ackerman, R. A., & Russell, D. W. (2009). Reporting and interpreting research in PSPB: Practices, principles, and pragmatics. *Personality and Social Psychology Bulletin, 35*(9), 1131–1142.

Peat, J., Elliott, E., Baur, L., & Keena, V. (2007). *Scientific writing: Easy when you know how*. Hoboken: BMJ Books.

Construct Clarity

Construct clarity refers to the extent to which the concepts we use are articulated precisely (Suddaby, 2010). The following articles provide greater attention to the significance of this issue and how to achieve concept clarity for improving measurement.

Gregory, J. B., & Levy, P. E. (2010). Employee coaching relationships: Enhancing construct clarity and measurement. *Coaching: An International Journal of Theory, Research and Practice, 3*(2), 109–123.

Johnson, R. E., Rosen, C. C., Chang, C. H. D., Djurdjevic, E., & Taing, M. U. (2012). Recommendations for improving the construct clarity of higher-order multidimensional constructs. *Human Resource Management Review, 22*(2), 62–72.

Organ, D. W. (1997). Organizational citizenship behavior: It's construct clean-up time. *Human Performance, 10*(2), 85–97.

Suddaby, R. (2010). Editor's comments: Construct clarity in theories of management and organization. *Academy of Management Review, 35*(3), 346–357.

Replication

Few replication studies have been conducted in social work research, which represents a major barrier in knowledge development. The following articles provide further justification for the importance of replication, including methodological issues that ultimately relate to measurement.

Hamermesh, D. S. (2007). Viewpoint: Replication in economics. *Canadian Journal of Economics/Revue Canadienne d'Économique, 40*(3), 715–733.

Hubbard, R., Vetter, D. E., & Little, E. L. (1998). Replication in strategic management: Scientific testing for validity, generalizability, and usefulness. *Strategic Management Journal, 19*(3), 243–254.

King, G. (1995). Replication, replication. *PS: Political Science and Politics, 28*(3), 444–452.

King, G. (2007). An introduction to the Dataverse Network as an infrastructure for data sharing. *Sociological Methods & Research, 36*(2), 173–199.

Bias in Scientific Research/Writing

As described in this chapter, publication bias is a serious problem to the advancement of scientific knowledge. Bias can creep in to any part of the scientific process, including measurement. Listed here are some general resources that will help you acquire a better understanding of research bias, which can help eliminate bias in all parts of the research process, including in the development, use, and interpretation of measurement.

Dickersin, K. (1990). The existence of publication bias and risk factors for its occurrence. *JAMA*, *263*(10), 1385–1389.

Dickersin, K. (1997). How important is publication bias? A synthesis of available data. *AIDS Education and Prevention*, *9*(1), 15–21.

Loannidis, J. P. (2005). Why most published research findings are false. *PLoS Medicine*, *2*(8), e124.

Olson, C. M., Rennie, D., Cook, D., Dickersin, K., Flanagin, A., Hogan, J. W. (2002). Publication bias in editorial decision making. *JAMA*, *287*(21), 2825–2828.

Shah, J., Shah, A., & Pietrobon, R. (2009). Scientific writing of novice researchers: What difficulties and encouragements do they encounter? *Academic Medicine*, *84*(4), 511–516.

Sterling, T. D., Rosenbaum, W. L., & Weinkam, J. J. (1995). Publication decisions revisited: The effect of the outcome of statistical tests on the decision to publish and vice versa. *The American Statistician*, *49*(1), 108–112.

Interpreting Research

Every interpretation of scientific data is determined by measurement. The following articles provide important perspectives on data interpretation, with an emphasis on effect size. We believe that effect size interpretation is an important contribution to the advancement of measurement. That is, validity arguments require substantive interpretations of correlations, as opposed to simply identifying associations that are significant statistically.

Cohen, J. (1994). The earth is round (p < .05). *American Psychologist*, *49*(12), 997–1003.

Gliem, J. A., & Gliem, R. R. (2003). *Calculating, interpreting, and reporting Cronbach's alpha reliability coefficient for Likert-type scales*. Columbus: Ohio State University.

Hemphill, J. F. (2003). Interpreting the magnitudes of correlation coefficients. *American Psychologist*, *58*(1), 78–79.

Hill, C. J., Bloom, H. S., Black, A. R., & Lipsey, M. W. (2008). Empirical benchmarks for interpreting effect sizes in research. *Child Development Perspectives*, *2*(3), 172–177.

Lipsey, M. W. (2005). The challenges of interpreting research for use by practitioners. *American Journal of Preventive Medicine*, *28*(1), 1–3.

Glossary

classical test theory, or CTT A body of psychometric theory used to understand and improve reliability of data derived from standardized measures.

classical validity theory A theoretical view that divides validity into different types and considers validity to be a property of the instrument.

coefficient of equivalence, or CE Used to assess specific factor and random response error; primary analytic strategies involve split-half, parallel forms, and internal consistency.

coefficient of equivalence and stability, or CES Used to estimate the magnitude of all three types of error (random response, specific factors, and transient); involves correlating two parallel forms of a measure on two different occasions.

coefficient of stability, or CS Used to assess transient and random response error but not specific factor error; the primary procedure is test–retest analysis.

Cohen's kappa (κ) A statistical estimate of interrater agreement.

concurrent criterion Used to correlate a measure of the focal construct with a criterion that has been measured at the same point in time.

confirmatory factor analysis A type of factor analysis that provides explicit tests of hypothesized structures; researchers make a priori specifications of which manifest variables or indicators are associated with the latent variable.

construct The theoretically defined concept, attribute, or variable that is the target of measurement; broadly covers the full range of measurement problems faced in social work research.

construct underrepresentation When a measure of a particular concept is too narrow or fails to include important dimensions or facets of the construct.

convergent–divergent/discriminative evidence An interpretation of validity made on the basis of empirical associations that are expected (convergent) and the absence of associations that are not expected (divergent; also referred to as discriminative) evidence.

criterion relationships An interpretation of validity based on the extent to which a measure agrees with another measure of the same construct; assessed with relational strategies, typically empirical correlations; *see concurrent criterion, predictive criterion, postdictive criterion*.

Cronbach's alpha The most commonly used statistic for estimating the internal consistency of a measure.

dimensionality Unidimensional measures characterized by item homogeneity.

domain-sampling model A model of measurement error that considers any particular measure to be composed of responses to a random sample of items from a hypothetical domain of items.

error In classical test theory, considered to be the difference between the observed values and the true scores.

error-free estimate An assumption that a variable is completely free of both random and systematic error.

exploratory factor analysis A statistical procedure used to explore or discover latent variables within a set of indicators, and to explore or discover the structure or dimensions (also referred to as subscales or factors) of a latent variable.

formative model Assume that measured variables define the latent variable.

generalizability theory, or G-theory A psychometric theory considered to be a liberalization of classical test theory; provides a framework for quantifying and distinguishing sources of inconsistencies in observed scores that arise or could arise over replications of a measurement procedure.

homogeneity Items of a measure that have a single common factor that have a linear relationship with the underlying factor.

idiosyncratic rater error A result of any of the three major types of error (i.e., random response, specific factor, and transient), but the source of the error is that of a rater in observational studies rather than a respondent to a scale, index, or exam.

indicators Observable entities that serve as the basis for measurement; also referred to as an item; can come in many different forms, such as a question to measure an ability, a statement to elicit a level of belief, a count of some specific behavior, and so on.

intercorrelation The correlations among the measured variable that is composed of multiple indicators.

internal consistency The interrelatedness among the items of a measure typically assessed using Cronbach's alpha.

interrater reliability The extent to which two or more raters exhibit agreement in ratings or assessments.

Interval-level measurement Mutual exclusive classification, magnitude ordering, and equal intervals between scale values.

intraclass correlation, or ICC The primary strategy for assessing interrater reliability when the level of measurement is at the ordinal, continuous, and ratio levels; a number of variants exist to account for multiple raters and different rating designs.

latent variable A feature hidden from direct observation or hypothetical constructs hypothesized to facilitate scientific explanation.

manifest variable Measured through one or more of the five human senses: sight, smell, taste, touch, and hearing.

measurement error In classical test theory, represents the difference between the observed scores and true scores.

nominal definition Giving a specific meaning, usually with synonyms or related concepts, to a construct; also referred to as a conceptual definition.

Nominal-level measurement Involves mutually exclusive classification; properties of symmetry and transitivity are assumed in nominal measures.

operational definition Indicates exactly what is to be observed, how the observations are to be made, and the assumptions governing the observations.

ordinal-level measurement Mutual exclusive classification and an order representing relative amounts or magnitude; in addition to the assumptions of symmetry and transitivity, assumes a single continuum underlying the classification or position of cases.

postdictive criterion Involves use of a previously measured criterion; similar to a predictive criterion.

precision The amount of information available, which infers the level of precision, and the relationships among the categories, scores, or values of a variable.

predictive criterion Used to correlate a current measure of the focal construct with a future outcome.

procedural assumption The relationships among the categories, scores, or values of a variable.

proxy variable Used as a substitute for another variable.

qualitative variable Measured at the nominal or ordinal level of precision.

quantitative variable Measured at the interval or ratio level of precision.

random error A class of errors (including random response, specific factor, and transient) not correlated with the construct, other measures, or anything else under study; distributed symmetrically around the true value, with some observed scores being greater than the true score and others being less than the true score; these errors balance each other out, making the expected value (mean score) a reasonable estimate of the true score.

Ratio-level measurement Mutual exclusive classification, magnitude ordering, and equal intervals between scale values, as well as a meaningful zero point.

reflective indicator model Assumes changes in the latent variable give rise to uniform changes in the manifest variables.

reliability The degree to which measurements are free from error, making reliability inversely related to error.

reliability coefficient Any one of a class of statistics that describes the reliability of the data based on a given measurement.

split-half reliability Dividing a measure in half randomly or systematically and assessing the extent to which each half is equivalent.

standard error of measurement, or SEM The amount of variation or spread of measurement errors from use of a measurement instrument; is useful for constructing confidence intervals around observed scores to help make the reliability of individual scores more interpretable; estimated by multiplying the sample standard deviation by the square root of one less the reliability coefficient.

standardized measure Any type of instrument (e.g., scale, test, inventory) administered and scored in a uniform and consistent manner.

statistical assumption Deals with issues of generalizing from samples to populations.

systematic error Exists when measures concentrate around alternative values instead of the true value; the observed scores are not distributed symmetrically around the true score; they are biased consistently upward or downward.

test–retest reliability Involves taking measurements on one occasion (time 1), repeating the measurement process at a later time (time 2), and then assessing the consistency of the responses across time using correlational procedures; assumes the meaning of the construct remains the same over the time period assessed.

theoretical assumption Involves the adequacy of definitions, comprehensiveness and representativeness of the indicators used to represent constructs, variability in the meanings associated with indicators, stability of meaning over time, and many others.

true score, or T In classical test theory, the expected value or hypothetical average score based on many trials of a measure or administrations of a measurement device, such as a scale.

unidimensional measure Composed of items that measure the same attribute—ability, achievement, opinion, or attitude—of a specified construct; characterized by item homogeneity.

validation The process of collecting validity evidence.

validity An integrated evaluative judgment of the degree to which empirical evidence and theoretical rationales support the adequacy and appropriateness of inferences and actions based on test scores or other modes of assessment.

validity evidence Different sources of information drawn together to support the inferences made from a given measurement.

References

American Educational Research Association, American Psychological Association, & National Council on Measurement in Education. (2014). *Standards for educational and psychological testing.* Washington, DC: American Educational Research Association.

American Psychiatric Association. (2013). *Diagnostic and statistical manual of mental disorders* (5th ed.). Washington, DC: Author.

Barman, A. (2011). Feasibility of applying classic test theory in testing reliability of student assessment. *International Medical Journal, 181*(2), 110–113.

Beck, A. T., Steer, R. A., & Carbin, M. G. (1988). Psychometric properties of the Beck Depression Inventory: Twenty-five years of evaluation. *Clinical Psychology Review, 8.1,* 77–100.

Beck, A. T., Steer, R. A., & Brown, G. K. (1996). Manual for the Beck Depression Inventory—II. San Antonio, TX: Psychological Corporation.

Beckman, T. J., Cook, D. A., & Mandrekar, J. N. (2005). What is the validity evidence for assessments of clinical teaching? *Journal of General Internal Medicine, 20*(12), 1159–1164.

Bergkvist, L., & Rossiter, J. R. (2007). The predictive validity of multiple-item versus single-item measures of the same constructs. *Journal of Marketing Research, 44*(2), 175–184.

Betty Ford Institute Consensus Panel. (2007). What is recovery? A working definition from the Betty Ford Institute. *Journal of Substance Abuse Treatment, 33*(3), 221–228.

Blalock, H. M. (1968). The measurement problem: a gap between the languages of theory and research. In H. M. Jr. Blalock, A. Blalock (Ed.), *Method ology in social research* (pp. 5–27). New York: McGraw Hill.

Blalock, H. M. (1984). *Basic dilemmas in the social sciences*. Beverly Hills: Sage.

Bollen, K. A. (1989). *Structural equations with latent variables*. New York: Wiley.

Bollen, K., & Lennox, R. (1991). Conventional wisdom on measurement: A structural equation perspective. *Psychological Bulletin, 110*(2), 305–314.

Borsboom, D. (2008). Latent variable theory. *Measurement, 6*, 25–53.

Borsboom, D., Mellenbergh, G. J., & van Heerden, J. (2004). The concept of validity. *Psychological Review, 111*(4), 1061–1071.

Brayfield, A. H., & Rothe, H. F. (1951). An index of job satisfaction. *Journal of Applied Psychology, 35*(5), 307–311.

Brennan, R. (2000). (Mis)conceptions about generalizability theory. *Educational measurement: Issues and practice, 19*(1), 5–10.

Brennan, R. L. (2006). Perspectives on the evolution and future of educational measurement. In R. L. Brennan (Ed.), *Educational measurement* (4th ed., pp. 1–16). Westport, CT: Praeger.

Brennan, R. L. (2011). Generalizability theory and classical test theory. *Applied Measurement in Education, 24*, 1–21.

Cabrera-Nguyen, P. (2010). Author guidelines for reporting scale development and validation results in the Journal of the Society for Social Work and Research. *Journal of the Society for Social Work and Research, 1*(2), 99–103.

Campbell, D. T. (1960). Recommendation for APA test standards regarding construct, trait, or discriminant validity. *American Psychologist, 15*, 546–553.

Campbell, D. T., & Fiske, D. W. (1959). Convergent and discriminant validation by the Multitrait–Multimethod Matrix. *Psychological Bulletin, 56*, 81–105.

Cattell, R. B. (1978). *Scientific use of factor analysis in behavioral and life sciences*. New York: Plenum.

Cizek, G., Bowen, D., & Church, K. (2010). Sources of validity evidence for educational and psychological tests: A follow-up study. *Educational and Psychological Measurement, 70*(5), 732–743.

Cizek, G., Rosenberg, S. L., & Koons, H. H. (2008). Sources of validity evidence for educational and psychological tests. *Educational and Psychological Measurement, 68*(3), 397–412.

Clark, L. A., & Watson, D. (1995). Constructing validity: Basic issues in scale development. *Psychological Assessment, 7*(3), 309–319.

Cohen, J. (1988). *Statistical power analysis for the behavioral sciences*. New York: Lawrence Erlbaum.

Cohen, J. (1994). The earth is round (p < .05). *American Psychologist, 49*(12), 997–1003.

Corcoran, K., & Fischer, J. (2000). *Measures for clinical practice*. New York: The Free Press.

Cortina, J. M. (1993). What is coefficient alpha? An examination of theory and applications. *Journal of Applied Psychology, 78*(1), 98–104.

Cronbach, L. J. (1950). Further evidence on response sets and test design. *Emotional and Psychological Measurement, 10*, 3–31.

Cronbach, L. J. (1951). Coefficient alpha and the internal structure of tests. *Psychometrika, 16*(3), 297–334.

Cronbach, L. J., & Meehl, P. E. (1955). Construct validity in psychological tests. *Psychological Bulletin, 52*(4), 281–302.

Davis, L. L. (1992). Instrument review: Getting the most from a panel of experts. *Applied Nursing Research*, 5(4), 194–197.

Diamantopoulos, A., Riefler, P., & Roth, K. P. (2008). Advancing formative measurement models. *Journal of Business Research, 61*(12), 1203–1218.

Diamantopoulos, A., & Siguaw, J. A. (2006). Formative versus reflective indicators in organizational measure development: a comparison and empirical illustration. *British Journal of Management, 17*(4), 263–282.

Diamantopoulos, A., & Winklhofer, H. M. (2001). Index construction with formative indicators: an alternative to scale development. *Journal of Marketing Research, 38*(2), 269–277.

Dickersin, K., Min, Y. I., & Meinert, C. L. (1992). Factors influencing publication of research results. *JAMA, 267*(3), 374–378.

Edelen, M. O., & Reeve, B. B. (2007). Applying item response theory (IRT) modeling to questionnaire development, evaluation, and refinement. *Quality of Life Research, 16*(1), 5–18.

Embretson, S. (1983). Construct validity: Construct representation versus nomothetic span. *Psychological Bulletin, 93*(1), 179–197.

Embretson, S. (2010). Cognitively based assessment and the integration of summative and formative assessments. *Measurement: Interdisciplinary Research & Perspective, 8*(4), 180–184.

Fanelli, D. (2010). "Positive" results increase down the hierarchy of the sciences. *PLoS One, 5*(4), e10068.

Feldman, R. A., & Siskind, A. B. (1997). Outcomes measurement in the human services. Washington, DC: National Association of Social Work.

Freese, J. (2007). Replication standards for quantitative social science: Why not sociology? *Sociological Methods & Research, 36*(2), 153–172.

French, D. P., & Sutton, S. (2011). Does measuring people change them? *The Psychologist, 24*, 272–274.

Friedmann, M. (1975). Interview with Richard Heffner on *The Open Mind*. http://www.thirteen.org/openmind/public-affairs/living-within-our-means/494/

Frisbie, D. A. (2005). Measurement 101: Some fundamentals revisited. *Educational Measurement: Issues and Practice, 24*(1), 21–28.

Gehlert, S. J. (1994). The applicability of generalizability theory to social work research and practice. *The Journal of Social Service Research, 18*, 73–88.

Gillespie, D. F. (1988). Barton's theory of collective stress is a classic and worth testing. *International Journal of Mass Emergencies and Disaster, 6*(3), 345–361.

Graham, J. R. (1987). *The MMPI: A practical guide.* Oxford University Press.

Green, S. B., Lissitz, R. W., & Mulaik, S. A. (1977). Limitations of coefficient alpha as an index of test unidimensionality. *Educational and Psychological Measurement, 37*(4), 827–838.

Guilford, J. P. (1954). *Psychometric methods.* New York: McGraw-Hill.

Guo, B., Perron, B., & Gillespie, D. F. (2008). A systematic review of structural equation modeling in social work research. *British Journal of Social Work, 39*, 1556–1574.

Hallgren, K. A. (2012). Computing inter-rater reliability for observational data: An overview and tutorial. *Tutorials in Quantitative Methods for Psychology, 8*(1), 23–34.

Hambleton, R. K., Swaminathan, H. Y., & Rogers, H. J. (1991). *Fundamentals of item response theory.* Newbury Park: Sage.

Hattie, J. (1985). Methodology review: Assessing unidimensionality of tests and items. *Applied Psychological Measurement, 9*, 139–164.

Haynes, S. N., Richard, D., & Kubany, E. S. (1995). Content validity in psychological assessment: A functional approach to concepts and methods. *Psychological Assessment, 7*(3), 238–247.

Heggestad, E. D., George, E., & Reeve, C. L. (2006). Transient error in personality scores: Considering honest and faked responses. *Personality and Individual Differences, 40*, 1201–1211.

Hinkin, T. R. (1995). A review of scale development practices in the study of organizations. *Journal of Management, 21*(5), 967–988.

Hogan, T. P., & Angello, J. (2004). An empirical study of reporting practices concerning measurement validity. *Educational and Psychological Measurement, 64*, 802–812.

Hogan, T. P., Benjamin, A., & Brezinski, K. L. (2000a). Reliability methods: A note on the frequency of use of various types. *Educational and Psychological Measurement, 60*(4), 523–531.

Hogan, T. P., Benjamin, A., & Brezinski, K. L. (2000b). Reliability methods: Frequency of use of various types. *Educational and Psychological Measurement, 60*, 523–531.

Howell, R. D. (2008). Observed variables are indeed more mysterious than commonly supposed. *Measurement: Interdisciplinary Research & Perspective, 6*, 97–101.

Hunter, J. E., & Schmidt, R. L. (2004). *Methods of meta-analysis: correcting error and bias in research findings* (2nd ed.). Thousand Oaks, CA: Sage Publications, Inc.

Jarvis, C. B., MacKenzie, S. B., & Podsakoff, P. M. (2003). A critical review of construct indicators and measurement model misspecification in marketing and consumer research. *Journal of consumer research, 30*(2), 199–218.

Johnston, M. (1999). Mood in chronic disease: Questioning the answers. *Current Psychology, 18,* 71–87.

Kane, M. T. (2001). Current concerns in validity theory. *Journal of Educational measurement, 38*(4), 319–342.

Kane, M. (2011). The errors of our ways. *Journal of Educational Measurement, 48*(1), 12–30.

Kashy, D. A., Donnellan, M. B., Ackerman, R. A., & Russell, D. W. (2009). Reporting and interpreting research in PSPB: Practices, principles, and pragmatics. *Personality and Social Psychology Bulletin, 35*(9), 1131–1142.

Kelvin, W. T. (1871). Presidential inaugural address to the General Meeting of the British Association, Edinburgh.

Kerlinger, F. (1968). *Foundations of behavioral research.* New York: Holt, Rinehart and Winston.

King, G. (1995). Replication, replication. *PS: Political Science and Politics, 28,* 444–452.

Kishton, J. M., & Widaman, K. F. (1994). Unidimensional versus domain representative parceling of questionnaire items: An empirical example. *Education and Psychological Measurement, 54*(3), 757–765.

Kline, P. (1979). Psychometrics and psychology. London: Academic Press.

Kline, R. B. (2010). *Principles and practice of structural equation modeling.* New York: Guilford Press.

Kline, R. B. (2012). Assumptions of structural equation modeling. In R. Hoyle (Ed.), *Handbook of structural equation modeling* (pp. 111–125). New York: Guilford Press.

Kuhn, T. S. (1962). *The structure of scientific revolutions.* Chicago: University of Chicago Press.

Loevinger, J. (1957). Objective tests as instruments of psychological theory. *Psychological Reports, 3,* 635–694.

Lord, F. M. & Novick, M. R. (1968). *Statistical theories of mental test scores.* Reading MA: Addison-Welsley Publishing Company.

MacKenzie, S. B. (2003). The dangers of poor construct conceptualization. *Journal of the Academy of Marketing Science, 31*(3), 323–326.

Madsen, D. (2004). Stablility coefficient. In M. S. Lewis-Beck, A. Bryman, & T. F. Liao (Eds.), *Encyclopedia of social research methods* (pp. 1064–1065). Thousand Oaks, CA: SAGE.

Marsh, H. W. (1996). Positive and negative global self-esteem: A substantively meaningful distinction or artifactors?. *Journal of Personality and Social Psychology, 70*(4), 810.

Mayfield, D., McLeod, G., & Hall, P. (1974). The CAGE questionnaire: validation of a new alcoholism screening instrument. *American Journal of Psychiatry* 131(10), 1121–1123.

Maxwell, J. C. (1870). Address to the Mathematical and Physical Sections of the British Association, Liverpool.

McCambridge, J. & Day, M. (2007). Randomized controlled trial of the effects of completing the Alcohol Use Disorders Identification Test questionnaire on self-reported hazardous drinking. *Addiction, 103,* 241–248.

McGrath, J. E. (1982). Dilemmatics: The study of research choices and dilemmas. In J. E. McGrath, J. Martin, and R. A. Kulka (eds.), *Judgment Calls in Research*. Beverly Hills: Sage, 69–102.

McGrath, R. (2005). Conceptual complexity and construct validity. *Journal of Personality Assessment, 85*(2), 112–124.

Messick, S. (1989). *Validity*. In R. L. Linn (Ed.), *Educational measurement* (3rd ed., pp. 13–103). New York: Macmillan.

Messick, S. (1995). Validity of psychological assessment: Validation of inferences from persons' responses and performances as scientific inquiry into score meaning. *American Psychologist, 50*(9), 741–749.

Mileti, D. (1999). *Disasters by design: A reassessment of natural hazards in the United States*. Washington DC: National Academies Press.

Mills, C. W. (1959). *The sociological imagination*. New York: Oxford University Press.

Mowday, R. T., Steers, R. M., & Porter, L. W. (1979). The measurement of organizational commitment. *Journal of Vocational Behavior, 14*(2), 224–247.

Muchinsky, P. M. (1996). The correction for attenuation. *Educational and Psychological Measurement, 56*(1), 63–75.

Mulaik, S. A. (1994). The critique of pure statistics: Artifact and objectivity in multivariate statistics. In B. Thompson (Ed.), *Advances in social science methodology* (pp. 241–289). Greenwich, CT: JAI.

Netemeyer, R. G., Bearden, W. O., & Sharma, S. (2003). *Scale development in the social sciences: Issues and applications*. Palo Alto: Sage Publications.

Nunnally, J. C. (1978). *Psychometric theory* (2nd ed.). New York: McGraw-Hill.

Nunnally, J. C., & Bernstein, I. H. (1994). *Psychometric theory* (3rd ed.). New York: McGraw-Hill.

Perron, B. E., Zeber, J. E., Kilbourne, A. M., & Bauer, M. S. (2009). A brief measure of perceived clinician support by patients with bipolar spectrum disorders. *The Journal of Nervous and Mental Disease, 197*(8), 574–579.

Raykov, T., & Marcoulides, G. A. (2011). Classical item analysis using latent variable modeling: A note on a direct evaluation procedure. *Structural Equation Modeling, 18*(2), 315–324.

Rogers, W. M., & Schmitt, N. (2004). Parameter recovery and model fit using multidimensional composites: a comparison of four empirical parceling algorithms. *Multivariate Behavioral Research, 39,* 379–412.

Rossiter, J. R. (2002). The C-OAR-SE procedure for scale development in marketing. *International Journal of Research in Marketing, 19*(4), 305–335.

Rozeboom, W. W. (1966). Scaling theory and the nature of measurement. *Synthese, 16,* 170–233.

Rubio, D. M., Berg-Weger, M., Tebb, S. S., Lee, E. S., & Rauch, S. (2003). Objectifying content validity: Conducting a content validity study in social work research. *Social Work Research, 27*(2), 94–104.

Schmidt, F. (2010). Detecting and correcting lies that data tell. *Perspectives on Psychological Science, 5*(3), 233–242.

Schmidt, F. L., & Hunter, J. E. (1996). Measurement error in psychological research: Lessons from 26 research scenarios. *Psychological Methods, 1*(2), 199–223.

Schmidt, F. L., & Hunter, J. E. (1999). Theory testing and measurement error. *Intelligence, 27*(3), 183–198.

Schmidt, F. L., Le, H., & Ilies, R. (2003). Beyond alpha: An empirical examination of the effects of different sources of measurement error on reliability estimates for measures of individual differences constructs. *Psychological Methods, 8*(2), 206–224.

Schmidt, F. L., Viswesvaran, C., & Ones, D. (2000). Reliability is not validity and validity is not reliability. *Personnel Psychology, 53*(4), 901–912.

Schumacker, R. E., & Lomax, R. G. (2004). *A beginner's guide to structural equation modeling.* New York: Lawrence Erlbaum.

Sellers, S.L., Mathesien, S., Perry, R., & Smith, T. (2004). Evaluation of social work journal quality: Citation vs reputation approaches. *Journal of a Social Work Education, 40*(1), 143–160.

Society for Social Work and Research. (2005). Peer review and publication standards in social work journals: The Miami statement. *Social Work Research, 29*(2), 119–121.

Stevens, S. S. (1946). On the theory of scales of measurement. *Science, 103*(2648), 677–680.

Streiner, D. L., & Norman, G. R. (2008). *Health measurement scales: a practical guide to their development and use.* Oxford University Press.

Suddaby, R. (2010). Editor's comments: Construct clarity in theories of management and organization. *Academy of Management Review, 35*(3), 346–357.

Thompson, B., & Daniel, L. G. (Ed.). (1996). Factor analytic evidence for the construct validity of scores: A historical overview and some guidelines. *Education and Psychological Measurement, 56*(2), 197–208.

Viswanathan, M. (2005). What causes measurement error?. In T. Alpern, M. Crouppen, L. Lech, L.C. Shaw, & M. Viswanathan (Eds.), *Measurement error and research design* (1st ed., pp. 135–148). Thousand Oaks: Sage.

Williams, L. J. & O'Boyle, E. H. (2008). Measurement models for linking latent variables and indicators: A review of human resource management research using parcels. *Human Resource Management Review, 18*, 233–242.

Worthington, R. L., & Whittaker, T. A. (2006). Scale development research a content analysis and recommendations for best practices. *The Counseling Psychologist, 34*(6), 806–838.

Index